STRANGE BUT TRUE
MISSISSIPPI

SWEETWATER
PRESS

Strange But True Mississippi

ISBN-13: 978-1-58173-550-5
ISBN-10: 1-58173-550-2

Design by Miles G. Parsons
Map of Mississippi by Tim Rocks

Printed in The United States of America

LYNNE L. HALL

SWEETWATER
PRESS

TABLE OF CONTENTS

In a Strange State:

Road Trip Through Strange But True Mississippi

What comes to mind when you think of Mississippi? Bet you think of grand antebellum homes, supported by stately white columns and decorated with Southern belles in brightly-colored hoop skirts; country lanes shaded by massive live oaks, their spreading canopies languidly dripping lacy tendrils of Spanish moss; or the scent of magnolia blossoms perfuming the humid air, while languorous ladies sip mint juleps on the veranda.

Or maybe you think of the talent Mississippi has spawned, some of the world's greatest. William Faulkner, Eudora Welty, Tennessee Williams, and John Grisham are just four of many talented writers who were born and reared here. Then, there's the music. The Mississippi Delta is the birthplace of the Blues and more than one hundred musicians got their start here.

That's the Mississippi the state's tourism department wants you to see. "It's Like Coming Home," they tell you. Read their colorful brochures, watch their slick commercials, and you'll see a state of tremendous natural beauty, populated by people of genteel culture and filled with magnificent sights. Stately, elegant, beautiful.

Ah, but there's another Mississippi lurking behind all that

loveliness and sophistication and it's a state of pure wackiness, filled with eccentric characters, crazy happenings, extraordinary, weird, and sometimes even spooky places, and some of the most bizarre landmarks ever built.

So drop that colorful brochure. Turn off the slick television commercial. And join us on a journey down the back roads of Strange But True Mississippi. It'll be like coming home—if home is, say, as eccentric as a Tennessee Williams play.

Strange Statues

We've Got Statues

Scattered willy-nilly across Strange But True Mississippi is an eclectic collection of quirky statues and monuments.

AFRICAN AMERICAN MONUMENT • VICKSBURG

It was a long time coming. This monument, erected in 2004, is the first tribute honoring black troops of the Civil War to be placed on any Civil War battlefield. The nine-foot monument depicting three figures—two Union soldiers and one civilian field laborer—was sculpted by artist Dr. Kim Sessums. The soldiers represent the African-descent first and third infantries that participated in the Vicksburg campaign. One soldier and the laborer are supporting the other

The African-American Monument is the first tribute to African-American troops of the Civil War to be placed on a Civil War battlefield.
Courtesy of Vicksburg National Military Park.

wounded soldier between them. The Union soldier looks forward, toward a new future of freedom, which he has helped to secure. The laborer looks back at a past of slavery and the wounded soldier represents the blood sacrifice made by African-Americans in battle.

During the Civil War, more than 180,000 African-Americans fought for the Union, comprising 9 percent of the Yankee fighting force. Despite the prejudice they faced from both Confederate and Union soldiers, the United States Colored Infantry fought valiantly, with twenty-nine receiving the Congressional Medal of Honor.

The monument is located within the Vicksburg National Military Park. Of the more than thirteen hundred statues and monuments located within the park, it's the only one to commemorate the sacrifice made by African-Americans.

Located at 3201 Clay Street.

AROUND TOWN CAROUSELS ABOUND • MERIDIAN

Falling in with a national trend that's seen fiberglass animal sculptures paraded through the streets of the country's biggest cities, Meridian recently launched its Around Town Carousels Abound project. In the outdoor public art project, life-sized fiberglass sculptures of carousel horses have been scattered throughout downtown Meridian, where they grace the grounds of government buildings, businesses, and private homes.

The carousel horse was chosen as Meridian's icon because the town is home to the Dentzel Carousel, the world's only remaining two-row stationary Dentzel menagerie carousel. Each

Around Town carousel horse is uniquely designed and commissioned by a local artist. In most cases, the design in some way reflects the business or entity that sponsored the horse, such as in the case of the Meridian Lauderdale County Public Library. Named "I Spy," the horse is painted with scenes and characters from children's literature.

The project is ongoing, with horses being sponsored and added on a regular basis. As of publication, more than fifty of the vividly-colored steeds were prancing downtown. The location and description of each is available at the Meridian/Lauderdale County Tourism Bureau located at 212 Constitution Avenue.

CATFISH ON PARADE • BELZONI

Heck, we didn't even know catfish could walk! But here they are, parading the streets of Belzoni! These aren't your everyday ol' mudcats, either. These cats are quite dapper fishes, dressed to the gills in bright colors and sophisticated duds. They've sashayed their way uptown and taken up residence outside a number of Belzoni businesses.

As the heart of Humphreys County, Belzoni has good reason to celebrate the catfish. With more acres of farm-raised catfish than any other county, Humphreys is billed as the Catfish Capital of the World. The finny little bottom feeders have had a huge impact on the town's economy. And, what better way to celebrate than with a parade?

The Catfish on Parade project, similar to the Meridian carousel horses project, consists of thirty-three creatively painted fiberglass sculptures designed by a number of local professional and amateur artists. Each was sponsored by a local business and was designed and named with its sponsor in mind.

Then there's the Blues Cat, which honors Mississippi's Blues musicians; the Money Bags catfish, sponsored by the local bank; the Butterfly Fish, sponsored by the Belzoni Garden Club; and the Delta Darlin' Queen of Fries, sponsored by the Delta Diner. Since the sculptures have been placed throughout downtown Belzoni, going on a catfish hunt is a fun way to explore the town.

MEDGAR EVERS • JACKSON

The struggle for African-Americans continued way past the ending of slavery in this country. Mississippi was at the forefront of the struggle for civil rights and Medgar Evans was one of its most valiant soldiers. Born and reared near Decatur, he served in the Army during World War II, where he fought in Normandy. After the war, he returned to Mississippi and attended Alcorn University, earning a degree in business administration.

Settling in Jackson, he became an insurance salesman, a job that exposed him to the extreme poverty of the African-American community. When the National Association for the Advancement of Colored People (NAACP) came to Mississippi in 1954 looking for recruits to help in the struggle for civil rights, Evers quickly joined up as the Mississippi field secretary. He recruited new members, participated in lawsuits to desegregate schools, and investigated racial incidents and assassinations.

A peaceful man who preached against violence, he, nevertheless, was passionate and fearless. He became a prominent voice in the Civil Rights Movement and by 1963 had become a target for segregationists. On the evening of June 11, 1963, white supremacist Byron de la Beckworth hid in the bushes near Evers's home. As Evers was exiting his car, Beckworth cut him down with one shot. Black and white leaders from across the country came to Jackson for Evers's funeral then gathered in Arlington National Cemetery, where he was interred with full military honors.

Beckworth was tried for murder twice in the 1960s, but despite the evidence against him, two all-white juries refused to find him guilty. Finally, in 1994—thirty-one years later—Beckworth was re-

Medgar Evers played a major role in Mississippi's civil rights movement.
Courtesy of Jackson CVB.

tried and found guilty of murder. He was sentenced to life in prison.

Evers's legacy is a continuing inspiration. There are tributes to him throughout the state, and especially in his hometown of

Strange Statues

Jackson, with his neighborhood on Missouri Road being designated as historical. The Jackson-Hinds Public Library System honors his memory with the Medgar Evers Branch, located on Medgar Evers Boulevard. A statue of Evers graces its grounds. The bronze sculpture depicts Evers as he was in life, a calm force for civil rights.

Located at 4215 Medgar Evers Boulevard.

FALLEN FIRE FIGHTER'S MEMORIAL • JACKSON

A number of heroes have fallen in Jackson, it seems. The original Jackson Firehouse of the Jackson Fire Department, which currently serves as the MetroJackson Chamber of Commerce, is an historic landmark with the original barn doors. (Remember? Way back when, fire engines were horse drawn.) In front of the building stands a memorial to Jackson's fallen firefighters. The bronze statue depicts a firefighter gently cradling a child, who dangles a teddy bear from one hand. A plaque on the pedestal features the names of all Jackson's fallen fire heroes.

Located at 201 South President Street.

WILLIAM FAULKNER • OXFORD

The stereotype of Mississippi as a state of near illiteracy is belied by the sheer number of great writers it has spawned. Nobel Prize winner William Faulkner tops the esteemed list. Born William Falkner (without the "u") in New Albany, Faulkner was reared in Oxford, where his sense of humor and talent for the characterization of the unique Southern personality were developed.

Faulkner's great-grandfather was William Clark Falkner, an important figure in North Mississippi, who served as a colonel in the Confederate Army and built a railroad. The town of Falkner in Tippah County is named for him. He set a family literary tradition by writing several novels and served as the model for Colonel John Sartoris in Faulkner's later works.

Bored with school, Faulkner dropped out around the sixth grade, but demonstrated early artistic talents, writing romantic poetry modeled after European poets. Turned down by the U.S. Army Air Force because of his height (five foot, six inches), legend

A statue of William Faulkner sits in Courthouse Square.
Courtesy of Oxford CVB.

has it that Faulkner applied to the British RAF, lying on his application about his birth date and place. Some believe this is when he added the "u" to his name in an attempt to sound British. Others think it was simply an editor's mistake that Faulkner chose not to correct. Faulkner did get into the RAF, but the war ended before he saw action, though he did let folks think he had fought, regaling them with stories of his exploits.

Strange Statues

Returning to Oxford, he enrolled in the University of Mississippi on a special bill allowing war veterans—even those without a high school diploma—to attend. He spent three years studying, but dropped out without receiving a degree.

Faulkner's first book of poetry was published in 1924, but was not well received. He moved to New Orleans in 1925 and began hanging out with the literary crowd of the day—Ernest Hemingway, Hart Crane, and Tennessee Williams. He also spent time traveling in Europe, often visiting the French café frequented by James Joyce, but he was too shy to approach the great writer.

Faulkner's first novel, *The Soldier's Pay*, based on his brief RAF service, was published in 1926, followed by *Mosquitoes*. Neither book was successful and his publisher was close to dropping him. By this time he had returned to New Orleans, where he took advice from writer Sherwood Anderson to write about his native region. He discovered that his "little postage stamp of native soil was worth writing about" and that he would not live long enough to exhaust the possibilities.

In his subsequent writings, Faulkner invented a whole cast of Southern characters and the imaginary Yoknawpatawpha County, then set about telling the true drama of Southern history, from its historical growth through a century and a half to its eventual decadence. His works explored the decay of the old South and addressed racial prejudice and the tragic relationships between blacks and whites of the South.

His most celebrated works include *The Sound and the Fury* (1929), *As I Lay Dying* (1930), *Light in August* (1932),

The Unvanquished (1938), and *Absalom, Absalom!* (1938). He also was a prolific short story writer and wrote screen plays as well. He was awarded the Nobel Prize for Literature in 1949 and received a Pulitzer Prize for his 1954 novel, *A Fable*.

An internationally-known figure, Faulkner traveled worldwide, representing the country in cultural events. He also became known for his moderate-to-liberal stand on school integration. His last years were divided between Charlottesville, Virginia, where he served as writer-in-residence, and Oxford. On July 6, 1962, at age sixty-four, he suffered a heart attack. He was buried at St. Peter's Cemetery in Oxford.

To commemorate its most famous son, Oxford officials commissioned a statue of William Faulkner. Installed on the occasion of his one hundredth birthday, the bronze sculpture sits on a bench at the entrance to City Hall, pipe in hand.

Located in Courthouse Square.

FROG FARM SCULPTURE GARDEN • HARRISTON

At the Frog Farm Sculpture Garden, a folk-art sculpture garden, you'll find lots of frogs. But these aren't your everyday slimy green frogs. Oh, no! These froggies are real works of art. There are big froggies and little froggies, blue froggies and green froggies, fat froggies and little skinny froggies. There are even froggies wearing clothes! And if, in the course of all that kissin', you fall in love, despair not. They're all for sale.

Located at 186 Old Highway 61.

Strange Statues

THE GOLDEN FISHERMAN • BILOXI

Stolen! In an act of thievery most foul, someone walked off with the beloved Golden Fisherman Statue of Biloxi. Well, OK, there was a little more effort involved than just picking it up and walking off, since the thing weighed more than a ton, but you get the picture. The statue was erected in 1975 to commemorate the fishing and seafood industries, which helped to put Biloxi on the map.

Sculpted by artist Harry Reeks, the statue was a sixteen-foot fisherman casting a net. It was made of a metal alloy and covered with 24-karat gold leaf, making it a sparkling wonder in the Mississippi sunlight. Despite the gilding, it wasn't really pretty. In fact, with its beaked nose and patchworked body, it was quite unattractive, but it was Biloxi's and Biloxi loved it. The statue's theft added insult to injury, for it was nicked while it lay sodden and broken, knocked from its pedestal by Hurricane Katrina.

Recovered! Biloxi's Golden Fisherman Statue was recovered in Alabama and was returned home just weeks after being stolen. Unfortunately, the alleged perpetrator, unaware that the statue's metal was an inexpensive alloy (maybe he thought it was real gold), had stolen it for salvage, and so, had dismembered it for transportation. At the time of publication, its fate was being considered. Write your Congressman! Start a petition! The Golden Fisherman must be returned to a place of honor!

Mississippi is in Africa. No, we're not confused. It seems that back in 1834, long before the Civil War, Prospect Hill Plantation owner Isaac Ross, decreed in his will that his slaves be freed and arrangements be made for their passage to the west coast of Africa. His estate was to be liquidated to give the ex-slaves a new start in the new country of Liberia. A court fight ensued, accompanied by a revolt by the frustrated slaves, but in 1840, the heirs finally honored Ross's wishes. "Mississippi in Africa" is the name the two hundred former slaves gave to their new home.

Here, they recreated the patrician lifestyle they had learned in Mississippi, building their own Greek Revival Plantations and soon found themselves embroiled in tribal warfare with native Africans. For the complete story, read *Mississippi in Africa* by Alan Huffman.

HINDS COUNTY COURTHOUSE • JACKSON

Look! Up there! It's a bird! It's a...oh, wait. It's a couple of statues. Atop the Hinds County Courthouse, you'll find thirteen-foot statues of Moses and Socrates. In case you're not up on your symbolism, Moses is the messenger of the law and Socrates is the interpreter.

407 Pasacagoula St.

Strange Statues

HOWCOTT MONUMENT • CANTON

This is not your usual Confederate monument. Oh, it looks like a normal monument—a twenty-foot granite obelisk standing within a hallowed cemetery. But it is unusual. See, the monument was erected between 1894 and 1900 by W.H. Howcott, who fought with Harvey's Scouts. The Scouts, a Confederate troop under the command of Captain Addison Harvey, were described by General William Sherman as a "bunch of hornets." They made life miserable for Union Troops.

Yeah, we know, that's not unusual. The unusual part is that Howcott erected the monument to honor black servants who followed their masters into battle and fought with Harvey's scouts. It's dedicated, in particular, to his own servant, William. Its inscription tells the story:

"To the memory of good and loyal servants who followed the fortunes of Harvey's Scouts during the Civil War. A tribute to my Faithful Servant and Friend, William Howcott, a colored boy of rare Loyalty and Faithfulness, Whose Memory I Cherish with Deep Gratitude."

Located on East Academy Street.

HOWLIN' WOLF • WEST POINT

Life may have begun quietly for Chester Arthur Burnett in tiny West Point, Mississippi, but after establishing himself as possibly the most electrifying blues performer in modern history, he sure went out howling. Born in 1910, Burnett was eighteen when a chance meeting with Delta Blues legend Charley Patton set him on a new life course.

Patton taught Burnett the basics of the Delta Blues style and for the next five years, Burnett farmed full time with his family and played the blues at weekend fish fries and get-togethers. When the family moved to Arkansas, Burnett met another influential blues musician, Sonny Boy Williamson, who taught him the harmonica. The two teamed up and Burnett abandoned farming for a career in music.

As they traveled the Delta playing bars and nightclubs, Burnett honed his performing style. Though never as technically proficient on the guitar as Patton, he took some of

West Point honors "Howlin' Wolf" Chester A. Burnett with a statue in the center of town.
Courtesy of the City of West Point.

Patton's performing tricks and made them his own. He rocked the juke joints, harmonica strapped on his neck and one of the first electric guitars in hand. An imposing figure at six-foot-three and three hundred pounds, he would often drop to his knees or lie on his back, whooping and howling. Bet you figured out this is where he got his nickname "Howlin' Wolf," huh?

Burnett started recording in 1951, after establishing himself as a radio personality in West Memphis, Arkansas. He recorded two songs for Sam Phillips then moved to Chicago, where a healthy rivalry with Muddy Waters was reputed to have spurred both musicians to their full potentials.

Making Chicago his home, he continued to tour and record. By the seventies, he was extremely ill, suffering from kidney failure. Even so, there were times in the studio when he would dig deep, tap into the old fire, and bring the house down. He died in a Chicago hospital in 1976. He was inducted into the Blues Foundation Hall of Fame in 1980 and in the Rock and Roll Hall of Fame in 1991.

Those aren't his only honors, either. In 1995, the town of West Point established the Howlin' Wolf Blues Society of West Point, Mississippi, Inc., a non-profit organization dedicated to promoting blues education in North Mississippi and perpetuating Burnett's legacy and the legacies of other blues greats. In 1997, the Society erected an eight-foot, laser-etched black granite statue of Howlin' Wolf. Showing the Blues legend holding a guitar, the statue stands in the town's center.

Located on the Kitty Dill Memorial Parkway.

Laura Kelly • Kosciusko

What's a superstar gotta do? Really, you leave your little hometown, become the number one talk show host of all time and an Oscar-nominated movie star, and make a billion bucks, but still you don't get a statue. It's a travesty, especially considering that some plain ol' citizen, who never did any of those things, got a statue. Well, obviously, Oprah didn't have a husband as devoted as Laura Kelly's.

Laura Kelly, you see, was nobody special. Well, except to her husband. That man positively doted on her, and when she died he was devastated. In his grief, he decided he must have a tribute to his beautiful bride. So he sent a photograph of her in her 1890s wedding dress to an artist in Italy, who sculpted her likeness into marble. The statue was erected in the family burial plot, where Kelly could see it from the upstairs window of his East Jefferson Street home.

Laura Kelly's husband erected this monument over her grave.
Courtesy of the Kosciusko/Attala Chamber of Commerce.

However, the statue was such a perfect likeness of his lost love that it hurt him too much to look at it.

Located in the Kosciusko City Cemetery.

JAMES MEREDITH • OXFORD

His name may not be as recognizable, as say, Martin Luther King, but James Meredith is no less a civil rights hero. In 1962, Meredith, then a student at an all-black college, applied for admission into the University of Mississippi. When his application was turned down, he took his case to court and won.

Strange Statues

His admission was so vociferously opposed by then-governor Ross Burnett that federal marshals were sent to escort Meredith inside the university on October 1, 1962. Violent riots ensued on the campus, resulting in two dead and forty-eight wounded, and President John F. Kennedy dispatched five thousand National Guard troops to restore peace. Because his requirements had been mostly completed at his previous college, Meredith graduated in August 1963, the first African-American to do so.

Meredith participated in later civil rights events, including leading the March Against Fear in 1966, where he was shot and wounded. But he later renounced his participation, saying the concept of civil rights was an insult, making second-class citizenry perpetual. "I was engaged in a war…and my objective was to force the federal government…into a position where they would have to use the United States military force to enforce my rights as a citizen." Mission accomplished.

Despite Meredith's objections over the need to celebrate his opening of the doors of higher education, the University of Mississippi has erected a life-sized statue of him. The statue, located between the library and the main administrative office, is posed as if striding toward a seventeen-foot limestone portal. Inscribed above the opening are the words "Courage," "Perseverance," and "Knowledge."

Mississippi State Memorial • Vicksburg

Yes, we're aware of the irony that the Mississippi State Memorial, which honors the actions of Mississippi troops in the

Siege of Vicksburg, follows the monument of a civil rights hero, but, hey, that's how it fell.

The Mississippi State Memorial is located within the Vicksburg National Military Park. Constructed of granite, it is a seventy-six foot obelisk with bronze work battle scenes around the base. At the front is a statue of Clio, Muse of History.

Located on Confederate Avenue.

ELVIS PRESLEY • TUPELO

Memphis may count him as their most favored son. The world may proclaim him as King. But Mississippi is the state that birthed him. Elvis Aaron Presley was born on January 8, 1935, in a two-room shotgun house in Tupelo, a house whose electricity came in the form of one outlet in the ceiling of each room.

Although his family was poor, Elvis had the privilege of a loving family, who gave him the benefits of a good Southern raisin'. This is where he learned his good manners, the respect for others, and the politeness that stood him in good stead throughout his life.

Reared in the church, Elvis's love for music began with a love for gospel, particularly black gospel, which rocked Mississippi churches on their foundations every Sunday morning. He began singing in the choir as a child and soon learned to play the piano and guitar. It was in Mississippi, in fact, that Elvis made his first stage appearance, winning a talent contest at the age of ten. And, well, the rest is history.

As you might imagine, Tupelo is quite proud of its most famous son. There are many tributes here, including his home, which is now a sort of shrine visited by thousands annually. Near the house is a bronze statue of Elvis at age thirteen, the age at which he left Tupelo with his family for Memphis.

Erection of the statue came about upon the suggestion of Elvis fans from Ireland. It depicts the young Elvis as one might have seen him in those days, clad in overalls with a guitar clutched tightly in one hand. It's a fitting tribute to a young Southern boy who united the world with his music and his charisma. Thank you. Thank you very much.

Located at 306 Elvis Presley Boulevard.

Tupelo has a bronze statue of Elvis Presley at age thirteen. Courtesy of Mississippi Development Authority/ Division of Tourism.

Natural and Manmade Wonders

Wackiness abounds on the byways of our Strange But True Mississippi. No sappy theme parks here. Instead there's a weird hodgepodge of natural and manmade wonders.

BAMBOO EMU FARM • MERIDIAN

At first glance, the eighty-acre farm looks like any other farm—covered in pastureland and dotted with copses of hardwoods, a nice little seven-acre lake on one end. But, that's where all similarity ends. For you won't find cows or pigs grazing out there. No. What you'll see are herds of giant birds. They're six feet tall and can run thirty miles an hour.

Visitors are welcome to tour the farm and visit the emus. You can learn all about 'em from egg to big bird. On your way out, stop by the gift shop and take home a few emu products or some emu meat. It's meat and supposedly even better for you than turkey.

Located at 3280 Lakeview Golf Course Road.

BLUES MURALS • LELAND

Music fans accept that the blues were born in the Mississippi Delta, beginning as the songs performed by slaves as they toiled in the heat of the Mississippi sun. They brought this

rich musical and oral tradition with them, using their songs to
lighten their spirits and tell stories, as well as a clandestine
means of communication, broadcasting news, and plotting
escapes.

Set as a music genre by the 1890s, the blues began to be
heard outside of the plantations, an amalgamation of rhythms
and tones of
many different
African tribes.
As blacks
began to
assimilate into
American
society, they
blended their
rhythms with
the white folk
traditions and
instruments.
This marriage

Blues murals can be found throughout downtown Leland.
Courtesy of the Highway 61 Blues Museum.

of the two cultures produced the blues and has been the basis
of popular music throughout the twentieth century.

With the blues came the birth of the juke joint, social clubs
where the music was played, adapted, and passed from place to
place. As the music became more popular, young musicians left
home for lives on the road. Charlie Patton was the first
Mississippian to emerge as a blues musician. Between 1897 and
1934, he traveled with another blues great, Eddie "Son" House

of Coahoma County, who introduced the now classic "bottleneck slide technique." Now a main feature of the blues, the technique is performed by sliding the neck of a bottle or another hard object along the guitar strings, producing a distinctive wailing sound.

Robert Johnson, blues' most powerful legend, ran away from his Hazelhurst home to learn the guitar from House. Legend had it that Johnson sold his soul to the devil for his extraordinary ability to play and sing the blues. Other Mississippi blues greats include Tommy Johnson of Crystal Springs, Skip James of Bentonia, Big Bill Broonzy of Scott County, Howlin' Wolf Chester Burnett of West Point, and, of course, one of the greatest, B.B. King of Indianola.

The town of Leland honors these pioneer musicians with a series of murals on several downtown buildings. Commissioned by the Leland Blues Project, the murals are painted by local artists and feature the greatest local and national musicians.

Located on Main Street.

CACTUS PLANTATION • EDWARDS

Well, this is a prickly situation. Billed as The World's Only Cactus Plantation, the Cactus Plantation has thirty-five hundred different varieties of cacti scattered around the grounds and in greenhouses. Who knew there were that many? There're also other succulents, colorful bromeliads, day lilies, and tropical foliage to see.

Located at 1088 Champion Hill Road.

Natural and Manmade Wonders

CAUSEYVILLE STORE • MERIDIAN

Stepping into the Causeyville store takes you a step or two back in time. The first building was built in 1869 and served as a trading post for settlers and the Choctaw until 1895, when a new building was constructed. At that point, the first building became a cotton warehouse and was turned into a garage during World War II.

The new building was a combination store/doctor's office, with the local country doctor, Dr. Billy Anderson, practicing in a side room. Dr. Billy was a jack of all trades, also serving as the postmaster and soliciting local telephone customers. He was the first to put in a telephone in the store.

Dr. Billy practiced medicine here until 1930. In the 1920s, a marble back bar and soda fountain were added. The store has passed through several owners through the years, finally being restored by the Hagood family and listed on the National Register of Historic Landmarks. Trod across the wooden stoop and into the store, and you'll find a scene straight

The first Causeyville Store was built in 1869.
Courtesy of Mississippi Development Authority/Division of Tourism.

out of the past, where original cases display wares. There are antique player pianos and nickelodeons, vintage movie posters, and a grist mill that grinds corn meal. In the back, you'll find a number of antiques for sale.

Located at 6129 Causeyville Road.

Cougar Haven • Grenada

Cougar Haven, a refuge for exotic cats, is the home of some of the rarest big kitties, including lions and tigers and cougars. The most prized possession is Freckles, the liger. No, that isn't a typo. Freckles is a liger, a cross between a lion and a tiger, and he's rare. Only eleven such animals are known to exist. You can visit with the cats and learn about their lives and their habitats. There's no admission fee, but a $2 donation per person is asked, with the proceeds going for the care of the cats.

Dentzel Carousel • Meridian

German immigrant Gustav Dentzel came to America in the 1850s and founded the carousel-making industry in Philadelphia, Pennsylvania. His family is generally acknowledged as the country's most gifted carousel manufacturers, with their horses shown in dramatic movement. Their designs became the hallmark of American carousels.

In 1896, Gustav built the extraordinary carousel for the 1904 St. Louis Exposition, which was later sold to the city of Meridian. In 1909, it was moved to Meridian's Highland Park. Its house is the only remaining original building constructed from a Dentzel blueprint. The park, the carousel, and the carousel house are listed on the National Register of Historic Places.

In a recent extensive restoration, the original colors and designs on the animals, chariots, and canvas paintings were discovered underneath layers of paint. All have been meticulously restored and today the Dentzel Carousel is exactly as it was the day it was first opened.

Located at Highland Park Drive and 19th Street.

DEVIL'S PUNCHBOWL • NATCHEZ

The Devil's Punchbowl is a giant depression in a Natchez bluff overlooking the Mississippi. The depression is a geological anomaly and no scientific explanation has been found for its existence. Throughout the years, the area has gained both a sinister and a golden reputation. Seems that way back in the olden days, thieves and pirates were plentiful in the Mississippi River and along the Natchez Trace, which runs through the area. It was thought that the thieves and pirates stashed their loot inside the Devil's Punchbowl for safekeeping.

One of the most notorious thieves to habit the area was Joseph Thomas Hare, a cruel and brutal man. According to legend, when Hare discovered his lady friend was stepping out on him, he ordered his men to bury her alive—nude except for the jewels he'd given her—in the Devil's Punchbowl. Some say her spirit appears to visitors, offering them her jewels if they will give her body a proper burial.

Located one mile north of Natchez at the junction of U.S Highway 61 and 84/98.

Did you know that the best, and most famous, snow sled is made in a state where snow is rarer than hen's teeth? Yep, this sled, which has become an American tradition—up North, we assume—is made by Blazon-Flexible Flyer, Inc., located in West Point. It's true! We wouldn't snow ya!

DUNN'S FALLS • ENTERPRISE

Irish immigrant John Dunn was a man who believed in getting what he wanted and in the mid-1850s, what he wanted was a water-powered grist mill. There was just one problem. The placid Chunky River was too tame to power a factory. Ol' John just diverted a stream seventy yards away and sent it cascading down a bluff into the river below. Voilà! Instant water power.

In 1860, Dunn built his water-powered cotton factory.

Once used to power a factory, Dunn's Falls is now a recreation area.
Courtesy of Mississippi Development Authority/Division of Tourism.

Natural and Manmade Wonders

The machinery for the factory had been delivered just as war was declared. The Confederate government confiscated the factory, and under Dunn's supervision, blankets, hats, and knives were manufactured here. During the war, another building was constructed to house a blacksmith shop, a distillery, and machinery for carding wool to make soldier uniforms. The mill and hat factory continued to operate for many years after the war.

Today, Dunn's Falls Water Park serves as a recreation area, with an 1857 grist mill that has been reconstructed on the site of the original mill. The original home site also remains. The mill pond is stocked with catfish and there are nature trails wending through woods filled with wildlife. Primitive camping is available.

Located at 6890 Dunn's Falls Road.

EMERALD MOUND • NATCHEZ

Emerald Mound is the second largest Native American ceremonial mound in the United States. Rising thirty-five feet high and covering eight acres, the mound was built by the Natchez Indians and used from around 1250 AD until 1700 AD. Experts believe the mound was, at least for a time, the main ceremonial mound for the Natchez tribe.

During its heyday, Emerald Mound probably hosted large religious and social gatherings for the Natchez tribe. Secondary flat-topped mounds on either end of Emerald were likely the base of a temple and residences for priests or rulers. The mound was the political hub for the tribe and served as a distribution area for goods. Excavations of the site, beginning in 1838, have uncovered such items as animal remains, ceramic fragments, and tools, giving archeologists insight into the everyday lives of the Natchez tribe.

Located 10 miles northeast of Natchez.

FIRST PRESBYTERIAN CHURCH OF PORT GIBSON • PORT GIBSON

This church, established in 1800, has a long and storied history, but that's not why it made our Strange But True tour. That reason would be the huge gold finger this church is giving to the heavens.

You see, back in 1828, Reverend Zebulon Butler persuaded the congregation to move the church to Port Gibson and was instrumental in the new church's construction. The reverend was a fiery preacher, whose favorite gesture was to point an admonishing finger skyward. So, in tribute to the reverend, a young local woods craftsman named

The First Presbyterian Church of Port Gibson was established in 1800.
Courtesy of Mississippi Development Authority/ Division of Tourism

Natural and Manmade Wonders

Daniel Foley carved a huge fist with the index finger pointing toward the heavens and had it mounted as the steeple on the new First Presbyterian Church of Port Gibson.

That original finger was consumed by the ravages of time, but a new one was erected—this time covered in gold leaf—in 1901. It's a glorious sight. The interior is just as interesting. It features an old slave gallery and chandeliers taken from the steamboat *Robert E. Lee*. And, hey, while you're there, be sure to check out Port Gibson, the town General Ulysses Grant decreed "too beautiful to burn."

Located on (where else?) Church Street.

FRIENDSHIP CEMETERY • COLUMBUS

"Where Flowers Healed a Nation" is what this cemetery is often called. The cemetery was established in 1849. During the Civil War, both Confederate and Union soldiers were buried here. On April 25, 1866, the ladies of Columbus honored the Civil War dead by placing flowers on the graves of both Union

Friendship Cemetery contains many monuments honoring those buried there.
Courtesy of Mississippi Development Authority/ Division of Tourism.

and Confederate soldiers. This is considered to be the first celebration of Memorial Day.

Located at 4th Street South.

> Mississippi leads the world in catfish farming. There are more than ninety-one thousand acres of catfish in the state producing more than 70 percent of the world's supply of farm-raised catfish.

FRIENDSHIP OAK • LONG BEACH

The Friendship Oak, located on the campus of the University of Southern Mississippi Gulf Coast, is one of the oldest and most magnificent oaks in the world. More than five hundred years old, the tree reaches fifty feet into the Mississippi sky, with a trunk circumference measuring eighteen feet, seven inches. Its canopy branches out 156 feet, providing a phenomenal sixteen thousand square feet of shade. That's a heck of a picnic shade.

Located on Highway 90.

GRACELAND TOO • HOLLY SPRINGS

If you're still all shook up over losing the King, hie yourself on over to Graceland Too.

You won't find the King there, but you will find the next best thing—the King's stuff! And, wow, what stuff! Credit cards! Lisa Marie's sippy cup!

Curator Paul McLeod's obsession with all things Elvis

started way back on October 17, 1954. He remembers because it was his birthday. Says he saw Elvis playing in Holly Springs, which was the first of 119 times that McLeod saw the King in concert. He's spent his life collecting, cataloging, and compiling the minutia of Elvis's life.

You won't have trouble finding the place, for McLeod's fixation includes Elvis's sense of the gaudy. Graceland Too, McLeod's antebellum home, though painted a sedate white, is surrounded by dozens of Christmas trees, all painted red, white, and blue. A whitewashed section of concrete wall fronts the yard, and the entrance is flanked by matching whitewashed lions. An American flag, wreaths, and other decorations adorn the walls.

Then you step inside. The place is floor to ceiling Elvis. We mean, literally, floor to ceiling. Elvis is plastered all over the ceiling. And that's just the beginning. McLeod is eager to show off the more than 10 million (that's what he says) items of Elvis memorabilia he's collected, a collection he says has been estimated at $10 million bucks by Lloyd's of London. Why, there's one record here that's worth half a mil alone!

Located at 200 East Gholson Avenue.

LA POINTE-KREBS HOUSE • PASCAGOULA

Also known as Old Spanish Fort for unknown reasons (it's neither Spanish nor a fort), the La Pointe-Krebs house is the oldest standing structure in Mississippi. Despite its grand-sounding name, it's not one of those elegant plantation homes that populates the South. It's the age of the structure and its unusual construction that makes it worthy of interest.

Built between 1772 and 1788, the original building was a two-room structure built by Simon dit La Pointe, a carpenter by trade. It's believed that it first served as a family residence while a larger home was built and then, later, as La Pointe's workshop. The present structure combines two unusual construction forms. The original two-room structure is made with thick walls of oyster-shell concrete, which is called tabby. A third room, added in 1820, was made in the traditional French colombage style. In this style, a mixture of mud and Spanish moss, called bousillage, is used to fill in the cracks and spaces between wooden uprights. Animal bones and pieces of pottery made by early Pascagoula Indians can be found in both tabby and bousillage.

The building passed to La Pointe's daughter, who married Hugo Krebs, a plantar, surgeon, and inventor. Now owned and managed by the city of Pascagoula, the home sits peacefully on the banks of the Pascagoula River. Recently restored, some walls have been left exposed to show the tabby and bousillage construction.

Located at 4602 Fort Drive on Lake Avenue.

The world's first heavyweight championship took place in Mississippi City in 1882 and was won by John L. Sullivan. A few years later, on July 8, 1889, Sullivan fought another heavyweight championship against Jake Kilrain in Richburg. The fight lasted an epic seventy-five rounds and was once again won by Sullivan. That fight was the last sanctioned bare-knuckle fight in the world.

Natural and Manmade Wonders

LONGWOOD • NATCHEZ

Dr. Haller Nutt was an extraordinary man. Son of wealthy plantation owner Dr. Rush Nutt, a successful inventor and scientist, Nutt followed in his father's footsteps, inventing, among other things, a specially-designed cotton press. He was a millionaire by the age of twenty and a multi-millionaire by thirty.

Nutt invested much of his fortune in several plantations in Louisiana and Mississippi, accruing a vast acreage that yielded an average of thirty-five hundred bales of cotton annually. In 1840, his fortune set, Nutt decided it was time to settle down and start a family. He married Julia Williams and later surprised her by purchasing the Longwood Plantation, a property she had fallen in love with after a visit there.

It wasn't long before the growing Nutt family outgrew the

Longwood features a Byzantine onion-shaped dome.
Courtesy of Mississippi Development Authority/Division of Tourism.

rambling home and decided it was time to start anew. Hiring Philadelphia architect Samuel Sloan, he began construction of another Longwood in Natchez. But this wasn't to be just any old plantation home. Oh, no! Nutt wanted something different.

So together, he and Sloan came up with a truly different design for Longwood. Using exotic features of Moorish architecture, such as an octagonal shape and a spire topped by a Byzantine onion-shaped dome, they designed a blueprint for a six-story, thirty-two room mansion. Nutt was pleased with the design, predicting that after the home was built, the octagon shape would become all the rage.

Construction on Longwood began in 1860. Work began and furnishings were on their way when, alas and alack, that little disagreement between the South and the Northern aggressors put an abrupt end to construction. Sloan's Philadelphia workmen dropped their tools and returned home to take up arms against the South. Longwood was left unfinished except for five basement rooms. All of Nutt's fancy things from France were seized by the federal blockade, with many becoming displays in today's national museums.

Nutt and his family moved into the rooms that were finished, hoping, no doubt, to finish their magnificent digs once the little disagreement was resolved. It was not to be. His assets were confiscated and his cotton plantations were burned. Broken, Nutt died of pneumonia in 1864. His family and their descendants occupied those five basement rooms of the unfinished house for more than a hundred years.

Today, Longwood is owned and operated by the Pilgrimage Garden Club, who had it declared a National Landmark. A tour takes you through the upstairs of the home just as it was back in 1861, with the original paint cans, scaffolding, and tools awaiting the return of workmen. The

Downstairs, where the family lived for so long, is filled with family heirlooms. It's a look into a family and into the changes wrought by the Civil War.

Located at 140 Lower Woodville Road.

MARGARET'S GROCERY AND MARKET • VICKSBURG

"Marry me Margaret, and I'll build you a castle." Those were the words of the Reverend H.D. Dennis back in 1979. Well, Margaret said "yes" and the Reverend made good on his promise...we guess.

See, back then, Margaret had a grocery store out on Highway 61. It was your typical country store—small and made of unpainted wood. Not anymore. Preacher, as folks called him, got busy and turned Margaret's Grocery into something much more...grand? Well, unusual, anyway.

A World War II vet who learned masonry from the Germans, Preacher fronted Margaret's Grocery with huge castle-like pillars and arches made of cinderblock, and painted them in alternating bands of red and white with some blocks of yellow thrown in every now and again. Atop the entrance pillar and archway, he placed a large double-sided eagle. Hand-painted signs proclaim the structure now to be Margaret's Grocery and the "Home of the Double-Sided Eagle Church."

Found objects and more homemade signs proclaiming God for all people—Jews, Gentiles, blacks, and whites—decorate the grounds. It's all overlooked by a red and white fifty-foot tower, which Dennis says the Lord kept telling him to build higher. Inside you'll find a glorious hodge-podge of religious icons juxtaposed with shelves of plain old grocery items. Outside you'll see the Chapel bus, a huge traveling church, outfitted with pews and a podium, where Dennis does a lot of his preaching. The bus is painted silver and is decorated with aluminum foil and duct tape.

Located at Box 219 Highway 61 (Route 4).

MISSISSIPPI RIVER

From the cold lands of Minnesota to the warm sea waters of the Gulf of Mexico, the Mississippi River flows through the heart of our country. The second longest river in the U.S., its influence began long before the first white man ever set foot on the continent. Early Native American tribes settled along its banks and built their complex farming and hunting societies. It was they who gave the mighty river its name: Mississippi which means "father of waters" in the Choctaw language. The name of these early tribes echo in the place names of the state: Natchez, Houma, Biloxi, Pascagoula, Tunica, and Yazoo.

As the white man moved in and took over, the river became the primary method of transportation. By the 1800s a new era had been ushered in and a whole new lifestyle was born, a life of river boats and river rats—people who spent their lives on the river. Time marched on and better modes of transportation ended the river boat era, though shipping on the river is still a significant part of the New Orleans economy.

Old Man River is no less inspiring today. The Mississippi has the third largest watershed in the world, behind the Amazon and Congo. Its basin covers 1.8 million square miles, including all or parts of thirty-one states and two Canadian provinces. At its highest elevation, it reaches 1,475 feet at Lake Ithaca in Minnesota. The lowest, of course, is sea level as it runs headlong into the Gulf.

The river moves more than 159 million tons of sediment annually, depositing it in the southernmost areas as it slows down before entering the Gulf. This deposition formed the Mississippi Delta region, which comprises 3 million acres of coastal wetlands and 40 percent of the country's salt marshes. This area packs a significant economic wallop, providing 18 percent of the country's oil supply and 16 percent of the country's seafood harvest, including shrimp, crab, and crayfish.

In addition to its economic impact, the Mississippi is an invaluable wildlife resource. In all, 260 species of fish—25 percent of all species in North America—call the river home. More than 326 species of birds use the Mississippi River Basin as their migratory flyway, and 40 percent of the country's waterfowl use the river during their spring and fall migrations.

PALESTINE GARDENS • LUCEDALE

Palestine Gardens was the dream of the Reverend Walter Jackson, who believed the Bible to be a "place book." He searched sixteen years for a place where he could build the land of the Bible for common folk to visit, finally settling on twenty acres in Lucedale.

Nearing his retirement from preaching, Jackson and his wife set out to build their dream land. Using spades and wheelbarrows, they toiled in the hot Mississippi sun, constructing a dam to form the Dead Sea. Despite a lack in masonry experience, Jackson had faith in his abilities. Block by block he worked, laying his foundation and throwing in his imagination, and slowly the historic villages of Jerusalem, Bethlehem, and Jericho took shape. Finally, in 1960, after seven years of hard labor, Palestine Gardens opened to the public, with more than thirty-two hundred visitors that first year.

And things only grew from there. Although Reverend Jackson and the missus have passed on to their reward, their legacy lives on. The gardens have been visited by folks from all the world continents. Well, except Antarctica.

You can walk from Jerusalem down the road to Jericho and visit Bethlehem, where the whole saga began. Trek past the historic cities and seas. And if, in your journey, you feel nearer to God, then the Jacksons' mission has been fulfilled.

Located at 201 Palestinian Gardens Road.

Between 1824 and 1847, Joseph Hold Ingraham of Natchez wrote and published eighty novels, approximately 10 percent of all novels published in the country during that period. Among his works is *Prince of the House of David*, the first successful Biblical novel.

THE PETRIFIED FOREST • FLORA

Mississippi's Petrified Forest—the only one of its kind in the eastern U.S.—was discovered before 1854 after erosion, washed away the sandy soil that had covered it for more than

Natural and Manmade Wonders

36 million years. The erosion, caused by years of farming, has left a magnificent canyon. Giant petrified logs lie at the bottom of the canyon.

The logs, once part of a huge forest, were washed downstream by an ancient, flood-swollen river. Although in just ten-foot sections now, the ancient trees once stood more than one hundred feet and are believed to have been as old as a thousand years when washed into the log jam.

Along the self-guided nature trail through the Petrified Forest, you'll find some unusual formations, such as the Frog. One of the six-foot-diameter petrified logs, It bears a striking resemblance to a squat, smiling toad. There's also the Caveman's Bench, a section of log that invites you to stop and take a quick respite.

After your tour, be sure to check out the Earth Science Museum, where you'll find an array of dioramas, black light displays, and a number of prehistoric fossils. Don't forget to stop into the gift shop on your way out for that perfect souvenir!

Located at 124 Forest Park Road.

THE SINGING RIVER • PASCAGOULA RIVER

The Pascagoula River is known world wide as the Singing River. It's a mysterious phenomenon, a strange music of sorts, that sounds like a swarm of bees in flight. Best heard in the late evenings of summer and autumn, the sound begins softly, barely heard at first, and builds, growing louder and nearer until it wraps the listener in its gentle lyricism.

There is, of course, a legend behind this odd song. It involves a couple of star-crossed lovers, and two enemy families. Sound familiar? Yeah, like Romeo and Juliet, Princess Anola of the Biloxi tribe and Chief Altama of the Pascagoula tribe fell in love, despite the fact that their tribes were enemies. Anola was betrothed to a chieftain of her tribe, but she ran away to the Pascagoula tribe to be with her true love, Chief Altama.

This enraged her spurned suitor of the aggressive Biloxi tribe. The Pascagoula tribe was gentle, not given much to warfare, but they swore to protect Chief Altama and Princess Anola, even if it meant death. They were attacked and were quickly overwhelmed by the Biloxi, who planned to enslave them. Faced with that prospect, the Pascagoula chose death. With their women and children leading the way, the tribe joined hands and began to chant the song of death as they waded into the river until every last voice was silenced beneath the waters.

Despite numerous scientific hypotheses on the origins of Pascagoula's strange music, no real explanation has been found. But who needs science? We know it's the Pascagoula's death chant being sung across the ages.

SPIRIT THAT BUILDS MURAL • HATTIESBURG

It's a mural of epic proportions. The concept and work of internationally known Hattiesburg artist William Baggett, the Spirit that Builds mural is the centerpiece of the Hattiesburg Public Library. It's painted on ten-foot-high panels of sandblasted stainless steel that stretch 167 feet around the library's atrium and hang suspended thirty feet in the air. In living color with "a mythological view of reality," the mural displays Hattiesburg's history from the days of the American Indian to the formation of Hattiesburg as a lumber town to modern days.

Located at 329 Hardy Street.

In 1839, the Mississippi legislature passed the first law in the English-speaking world protecting the property rights of married women. Mississippi College in Clinton was the first coed college in the U.S. to grant a degree to a woman. The country's first rural mail carrier was Mamie Thomas, who delivered mail by buggy to the area southeast of Vicksburg in 1914. Burnita Matthews of Hazelhurst was the first woman federal judge in the U.S. She served in Washington, D.C.

STAINED GLASS MANOR • VICKSBURG

The Stained Glass Manor is the last home built by the Vick family, for whom Vicksburg is named. Built between 1902 and 1908, the home is thought to have been designed by George W. Maher, the Father of Indigenous Architecture. The National Register of Historic places calls it "possibly the finest example of Mission Architecture in Mississippi."

The most spectacular features of the magnificent home, now operated as a bed and breakfast, are its thirty-eight stained glass windows that cast an ethereal glow as sunlight filters through the gold, rose, salmon, blue, and green panes. Considered works of art, these windows were made by Louis J. Millet, the first dean of architecture at the University of Chicago and head of the Art Institute. Also called Oak Hall, the manor is known for its rich interior woodwork, elegantly-appointed furnishings, and spectacular staircase.

Located at 2430 Drummond Street.

TUPELO BUFFALO PARK • TUPELO

At the Tupelo Buffalo Park you can take the giant Bison Bus through the countryside, where you'll get up close and personal with the largest herd of buffalos east of the Mississippi. You're allowed

Buffalo roam in Tupelo.
Courtesy of Mississippi Development Authority/Division of Tourism.

to get out of the bus and feed these giant animals of the Old West. You'll also be greeted by many of the park's other exotic animals, including Charlie the camel, Patches and Freckles the giraffes, and zebras Zeke and Zelda.

Natural and Manmade Wonders

The park's prize animal is Tukota, the white buffalo. White buffalos are rare, occurring only once in 5 million births. They were so rare, the Sioux tribes believed the white buffalo to be the most sacred creature alive. Tukota was named by a local elementary school class, who combined the first two letters of Tupelo with the last letters of the tribes that so revered the animal. Pretty smart, huh?

There is a petting zoo and pony rides and, if you're really into it, you can arrange to spend the night at the park's Choctaw Indian Village.

Located at 2272 North Coley Road.

WINDSOR PLANTATION • PORT GIBSON

Stately columns are all that remain, but their size and number lend a suggestion of the magnificent home they once supported. Windsor Plantation, the home of wealthy planter Smith Coffee Daniell II, was built between 1859 and 1861. With its sumptuous furnishings, grand Corinthian columns, and wrought iron interior staircase, the elaborate four-story house reflected the pinnacle of grand Southern living.

During the Civil War, Confederate troops atop the home's observatory roof used signaling equipment to warn of Yankee troops advancing up the Mississippi River. A Yankee soldier was shot in the front doorway. Later, the house was occupied by Union forces, which used it as a hospital and an observation post, the most likely reason it was spared.

After the war, Mark Twain often stood in the observatory gazing out over the Mississippi River, perhaps ruminating on his next book. Twain wrote of Windsor in his tome *Life on the Mississippi*, likening it more to a college than a home because of its size.

Windsor survived the devastation of the Civil War only to be destroyed by carelessness of a party guest, who tossed a cigarette into a waste basket. According to records, the family was planning a seated dinner on February 17, 1890, but had left to pick up the mail. When they returned around three o'clock in the afternoon, flames were shooting from the roof. The conflagration burned the house to the ground, leaving only the twenty-three columns to mark its existence.

Columns are all that remain of the once magnificent Windsor Plantation. Courtesy of Mississippi Development Authority/Division of Tourism.

Many years after its destruction, the exact design of the house had been forgotten, though many artists endeavored to imagine what it would have looked like. Then came the serendipitous discovery of a diary in the Ohio State Archives in Columbus, Ohio. The diary belonged to Union officer Henry Otis Dwight, who had rendered a drawing of Windsor in its heyday, drawn on May 1, 1863.

Natural and Manmade Wonders

The ruins of Windsor Plantation have appeared in several feature films, including the 1957 movie Raintree Country, starring Elizabeth Taylor and Montgomery Cliff. A visit to the ruins, twelve miles outside of Port Gibson, will give you just a hint of past grandeur.

Strange Museums

There's a strong sense of history here, as evidenced by the large number of museums throughout the state. But you won't find works by Picasso or Monet gracing these walls. Nah. We're much more interesting than that.

AUTOMOBILE MUSEUM • TUPELO

You don't have to be a car nut to enjoy a tour of this museum, but if you are, wow! You'll be in heaven. The collection includes more than one hundred rare antiques, representing one hundred years of automotive design and engineering.

The exhibit begins in 1886, with the Benz, a funny-looking machine designed by Karl Benz in Mannheim, Germany. Essentially a two-person carriage seat mounted on three wheels, it was the first petrol powered device. And, it's just the beginning.

Through the next one hundred years, you'll find an amazing collection of rare machines, including such finds as a 1905 Glyde, a 1928 Hispano Suiza, and a 1929 Dusenburg "J." There're also celebrity and movie cars, such as a Lincoln once owned by Elvis and a DeLorean like the one in *Back to the Future*.

The cars follow chronological order and each features an audio presentation. In addition, the museum features an open restoration garage, where you can watch as experts work on cars that will soon be placed on exhibition. There are vintage automotive signs throughout and a full-sized reconstructed 1920s service station. Varoom! Varoom!

Located at 1 Otis Drive.

Settled in 1722, Rodney, a bustling river town, was considered the capital of Mississippi. It had the state's first opera house, more than thirty-five stores, and more than five thousand residents. Andrew Jackson was a frequent visitor and Zachary Taylor was living there when he won the Presidency.

During the Civil War, a group of wily Rodney citizens invited the officers of a Union gunboat docked in the harbor to church. When they accepted, the Confederates captured them. The gunboat fired on the town, but when the Confederates threatened to hang the officers, the crew backed off. A cannonball remains in the brick work of the old Rodney Presbyterian Church.

By 1827, the Mississippi River changed course, leaving Rodney high and dry. No longer a bustling river town, Rodney lost its importance, and most of its citizens moved away. Today, it's essentially a ghost town with just a few hundred residents remaining.

BEIDENHARN COCA-COLA MUSEUM • VICKSBURG

There's nothing we Southerners like better than a good ol' bottle of cold Coca-Cola on a hot summer day. And we have Southerners to thank for that particular treat.

Coca-Cola was first concocted by Atlanta pharmacist Dr. John Pemberton, who brewed the formula in a three-legged brass kettle in his backyard. Pemberton was no stranger to this type of formulation. His previous formula—Pemberton's French Wine Coca—sold as a nerve tonic, stimulant, and headache remedy. It was a stimulant all right. The formula contained cocaine, derived from the coca plant and caffeine from kola nuts. Sweetened with wine, it packed quite a punch, and was ever-so-popular, sold by most of the city's druggists. Cocaine, at the time, was legal and was sold over the counter at most drug stores.

Prohibition threw a wrench in Pemberton's little enterprise, however. Pemberton reformulated, using sugar as a sweetener instead of wine, but keeping that kick from cocaine. His bookkeeper, a man with a marketing future, no doubt, came up with the name Coca-Cola, and being a talented calligrapher as well, he fashioned the distinctive Coca-Cola script the company still uses today.

On May 8, 1886, Pemberton delivered the new formula to Jacob's Pharmacy in Atlanta, where once again it sold as a cure for "all nervous inflictions—Sick Headache, Neuralgia, Hysteria, Melancholy, Etc."

Spurred by a public backlash against cocaine in the 1890s, Pemberton once again changed the formula, still using the coca plant for flavoring, but now using denatured leaves, from which all the cocaine had been extracted.

Pemberton began distributing his Coca-Cola syrup to other companies across the South for distributions in soda fountains.

Strange Museums

One of those companies was the Beidenharn Candy Company of Vicksburg. Opened in 1890, the company was owned by Joseph Beidenharn and was located on Washington Street. One side of the store was the candy company and the other side was a shoe store owned by Joseph's father.

Beidenharn was impressed with the sales of Coca-Cola from the soda fountains in his store, and it got him to thinking: Why not bottle the stuff and sell it to the country folk? After getting permission from the Coca-Cola Company, who was uninterested in bottling, Beidenharn used the bottles from his soda water bottling business and began bottling Coca-Cola.

These first bottles, called Hutchison Bottles, were clear glass with a rubber disk that was pushed into the top and held with a wire. They were used only a short time, for the rubber disk changed the taste of the drink after about a week. In the early 1900s, Beideharn switched to a straight-sided bottle sealed with a crown, which preserved the flavor of the drink. By 1910, Beidenharn switched to a machine-made bottle that was more uniform in color and shape. They were embossed with "Beidenharn Candy Company, Vicksburg, Miss." "Coca-Cola" appeared in script across the base.

By 1913, Beidenharn's Coca-Cola bottling scheme was booming and the Coca-Cola Company finally decided it was time to jump in. They also decided the company needed a distinctive bottle to foil the efforts of imitators. They came up with the design and gained the first U.S. patent on a bottle. Today, Coca-Cola is the world's largest soft drink company, with 48 percent of the market share and four hundred products.

At the Beidenharn Coca-Cola Museum, located in the original building, you'll find a plethora of exhibits chronicling the history of the Coca-Cola Company. In addition, you'll see the history of the Beidenharn family, the process and equipment first used to bottle Coca-Cola, and Coca-Cola memorabilia on display and for sale.

Located at 1107 Washington Street.

BIRTHPLACE OF THE FROG EXHIBIT • LELAND

As a little tadpole, one of the world's best loved heroes paddled around in the calm waters of Deer Creek and, later, hopped along its muddy banks. As a youngster, he quickly learned the difficulties he would face in life, but like a true hero, he never let it get him down. Yes, it's not easy being green. But why wonder why? Green is all there is to be. And, green or not, our young hometown hero was destined for greatness.

I guess by now you've figured out we're talking about celebrity and world traveler Kermit the Frog, the creation of puppeteer and Leland's favorite son Jim Henson. Henson was born in Greenville in 1936, and spent his formative years in Leland. Growing up in the Mississippi countryside, he loved to ride horses and spend time fishing on the banks of Deer Creek with his best friend Kermit Scott. The beauty of those days stayed with him long after his family had left the South.

Henson's magic began early. While still attending high school in Maryland, he began working for a local television station, creating puppets for a children's show. The next year, while attending the University of Maryland, he created *Sam and*

Friends, a five-minute puppet show for WRC-TV and it was here that Kermit the Frog was born.

Kermit became Henson's signature character, and he, along with companions Rowlf the dog, Miss Piggy, Big Bird, Oscar the Grouch, Cookie Monster, and dozens more, changed the world of puppetry, so much so that a new name was required. Henson coined the word "Muppet" by combining marionette and puppet.

The Muppets and the world sustained a great loss when Jim Henson died of a deadly bacterial infection. At his funeral, Kermit held a place of honor seated on the coffin with a small sign, "I lost my voice." During the service, Henson's partner Frank Oz, the voice of Fozzie Bear, held up his Muppet and began singing "Just One Person," a favorite Henson song. In the audience, all the Muppeteers held up their Muppets and joined in. Big Bird came down the aisle and all the Muppets joined him in his trek to the front of the cathedral, where they concluded the song. It was a moving and fitting memorial to a man who gave life to a world of magic.

And that magic lives on. The Birthplace of the Frog Exhibit is a small museum housed in the Washington County Tourist Center/Leland Chamber of Commerce in Leland. The exhibit, donated by the Jim Henson Company, features a tableau honoring the birth of Kermit the Frog on Deer Creek, photographs from the Henson Family Album, a video center with early works by Henson, and a gift shop. A separate room contains a plethora of Muppet memorabilia.

Located on the bank of Deer Creek.

JERRY CLOWER MUSEUM • LIBERTY

It's fitting that Jerry Clower got his start as a comedian while working as a fertilizer salesman. As he traveled around, making his presentations, he'd tell funny tales as an ice breaker, a ploy that ultimately increased his sales. When a customer remarked that he might have a future in comedy, it got ol' Jerry to thinking.

Taping his next few presentations, he sent the tape to the WSM radio station in Nashville and things just broke loose from there. Soon, Clower, at age forty-five, found himself appearing on the stage of the Grand Ol' Opry and making hot-selling comedy records. It wasn't long before the whole country was laughing at Clower's tales and drawling, "Knock 'em out, Johhhn!"

Born in Liberty and reared in Yazoo City, Clower told true tales of his life, talking about these places. He may have embellished just a bit, but his stories were based on real-life events that occurred to him, real-life friend Marcel Ledbetter, and a whole cast of local characters. Clower was deeply religious and prided himself on tellin' tales the whole family could listen to. He was frequently asked to speak at worship services. His recording, *Ain't God Good*, was, in fact, recorded during one such service.

In his career that spanned more than twenty years, Clower made twenty-seven full-length recordings and authored four books. He was a member of the Grand Ol' Opry and performed there regularly. His book, also titled *Ain't God Good*, became the basis of an inspirational documentary, which won an award from the New York International Independent Film and Video Festival.

Clower died in 1998 at age seventy-one, but his humor lives on. The Jerry Clower Museum in Liberty contains memorabilia from his more than twenty-year career.

Located at 1 Amazing Grace Lane.

DELTA BLUES MUSEUM AND THE BLUES CROSSROADS • CLARKSDALE

Avid blues fans know the Robert Johnson song "Cross Roads Blues," where Johnson fell to his knees and begged the Lord to "save poor Bob, if you please." There's also the legend of how Johnson met the devil at a certain crossroads and traded his soul for his extraordinary musical talents.

Well, guess what? This is that crossroads! At least plenty of knowledgeable people think so. According to blues history, Clarksdale and the junction between Highways 61 and 49 are where the blues were birthed. With the Chicago, Illinois Railroad passing through, Clarksdale was a large business hub. It was here that countless blues musicians gathered and played their music until it was time for them to catch that blues train on to bigger things.

The crossroad is more of a junction where Highways 61 and 49 merge into a "Y," but Clarksdale marks it clearly with a set of electric-blue guitars mounted on a tall pole. Can't miss it. It's right next to the Church's Chicken. But take your time getting there, for the town is packed with blues landmarks, including the Riverside Hotel where the Empress of Blues, Bessie Smith, died after being injured in an auto accident.

To really immerse yourself in the blues legend, be sure to check out the Delta Blues Museum. Housed in the old Yazoo and Mississippi Railroad freight depot, it is Mississippi's oldest music museum.

Located at 1 Blues Alley.

INTERNATIONAL MUSEUM OF MUSLIM CULTURE • JACKSON

OK, you gotta admit that Jackson, Mississippi, is probably the last place you'd expect to find any museum on Muslim culture, much less the country's only museum on Muslim culture. But, here it is.

The museum was opened in 2000 by a group of Jackson Muslims as a way to educate the public about Islamic history and culture and the contributions of Muslims to world civilization.

They hoped, as well, to increase the appreciation for the diversity of Mississippi cultural and religious history and the role Muslims have played in the state's history and development. Through the

The International Museum of Muslim Culture educates the public on Islamic history and culture.
Courtesy of Mississippi Development Authority/Division of Tourism.

exhibits, the museum seeks to foster religious and cultural tolerance and reduce religious and racial bigotry.

Located at 117 East Pascagoula Street.

> The Mississippi River is the country's great dividing line. It's commonly used as a tool for dividing the U.S. into eastern and western sections, with places being described as east or west of the Mississippi. Additionally, most FCC call signs start with "W" east of the Mississippi and "K" on the west side.

CASEY JONES RAILROAD MUSEUM STATE PARK • VAUGHN

John Luther "Casey" Jones was a legendary train engineer, who, according to legend, sacrificed his life to save the lives of his passengers. Of course that's not everyone's take on the tale. Seems the official accident report settles the blame for the wreck that killed him entirely on Jones's broad shoulders.

On that fateful night—April 29, 1900—Jones had come into Memphis on the northbound Cannonball route from Chicago, on time, of course, and was looking forward to an evening at home. But when he learned a fellow engineer was sick and was unable to make his run, Jones agreed to take the southbound route to New Orleans on two conditions: That he drive the 382, his regular powerful engine, and that he have Sim Webb, his favorite fireman.

With both conditions met, Jones set out for Canton, Mississippi, almost two hours behind schedule. Ahh, but not for long. You see, he had a fast engine, a good fireman, and a light train, all the conditions needed for a record-setting run. By highballing (going fast and taking risks) the whole way, he knew he could make up lost time and maybe break a record or two. And, by golly, he would've, too, except for that one itty bitty problem. He squealed his way around a corner just outside of Vaughn, Mississippi, and what to his wondering eyes should appear, but a stalled freight train and six great big train cars. Knowing he'd never be able to stop in time, he screamed for his fireman to jump and save himself, and grabbed the whistle cord in one hand, the brake in the other.

Now here's where the legend gets a bit iffy. You see, once the brake's set, there's not much else an engineer can do, and Jones could've jumped to safety and the outcome would've pretty much been the same. But he stayed, heroically, many say, hoping to do something more to save his passengers. Guess it worked, since Jones was the only one to die that day. Legend has it that when he was removed from the engine, one hand was still clutching the whistle and the other held fast to the brake.

After the wreck, Jones was immortalized in a song, "The Ballad of Casey Jones," by Wallace Sanders, a friend of Jones's. The song found its way to vaudeville and by the end of World War I, Jones had become a legend.

The Casey Jones Railroad Museum State Park commemorates the life of Casey Jones and pays tribute to the history of railroading in Mississippi. Located near the site where the fateful crash occurred, the museum houses photos, archives, and other railroad displays.

Located at 10091 Vaughn Road.

Strange Museums

Landrum's Country Homestead and Village • Laurel

It takes a village to really give you an idea of what life was like a hundred years ago. Scattered throughout ten picturesque acres of pecan trees, streams, and lush foliage, you'll find the re-creation of an 1870s country village. In the sixty buildings and displays are cabins, a chapel, the general store, and the town jail. There's also a working gem mine, where you can pan for jewels, and a working 1871 grist mill.

Located at 1356 Highway 15 South.

Manship House Museum • Jackson

Charles Manship was born and reared a Yankee, but in the 1830s, he discovered paradise and never left. An ornamental painter, Manship came to Jackson to take advantage of the building boom. He found work on the construction of the State House, now the Old Capitol Building, and later opened his own shop offering paints and fine wallpaper.

Manship held several offices, including the office of mayor during the Civil War. In 1857, he built a home to accommodate his large family of fifteen children. Not content to be like everyone else, he bucked the trend of Greek Revival architecture and, instead, built a Gothic Revival country villa. Manship adapted the design, which he took from a popular nineteenth century pattern book, for the Southern climate by adding floor to ceiling windows and a central hallway that aided ventilation.

The state endeavored to restore the home to its condition in the year 1888. The original exterior olive drab color with cream trim was discovered beneath layers of paint and was faithfully reproduced. Inside, examples of Manship's decorative painting and wood graining survived and have been restored by master craftsmen.

Although Jackson has grown up around it, the Manship Home nestles on its original four-acre lot in a setting of native shrubs and trees, many of which were planted by Manship. Inside, the home is an accurate picture of what life was like during the late 1800s, complete with seasonal changes, such as "Summer Dress," when the annual spring cleaning was performed and the

Charles Manship built this home to accommodate his family of fifteen children.
Courtesy of Mississippi Development Authority/Division of Tourism.

home was prepared for the long, hot summer.

Located at 420 East Fortification Street.

MISSISSIPPI ENTOMOLOGICAL MUSEUM • STARKVILLE

Eww! Bugs! Lots and lots of bugs! There are more than a million of 'em and more than thirty-five thousand are being added annually. Thank goodness they're all dead! You'll find every kind of bug you could imagine here, from the plain old everyday house fly to the beautiful exotic butterflies from around the world. Little boys will be in bug heaven.

The Mississippi Entomological Museum houses every type of insect imaginable.
Courtesy of Mississippi Entomological Museum, Mississippi State University.

Visitors can view displays in the foyer of the Clay Lyle Entomology Building on the University of Mississippi campus, weekdays from eight a.m until five p.m.

ETHEL WRIGHT MOHAMED STITCHERY MUSEUM • BELZONI

Ethel Wright Mohamed was quite the whiz with a needle. But she was much more than a seamstress. She was an artist. When Mohamed picked up her needle, it wasn't to hem a skirt or mend a seam. It was to create beautiful pictures that told the story of her life.

Mohamed was born Ethel Wright in 1906 in Webster County. Her mother taught her to embroidery early in life, using it as a preoccupation for the child's precociousness. In 1924, Ethel married Hassan Mohamed, a Lebanese-born businessman. The couple moved to Belzoni, where their life was full, with eight children, a successful business, and an abiding love for each other.

They weathered the Great Depression and both World Wars together, building a great store of wonderful memories. But tragedy struck in 1965, when Hassan died after a long illness. Alone for the first time in her fifty-nine years, Ethel kept her days full running the store. But the nights alone were torturous.

So in the dark of lonely nights, she picked up her needle and began to paint pictures with her colorful threads. At first only showing them to family members, she later began displaying her pictures in local art exhibits, where her work was discovered by representatives of the Smithsonian Institute.

Soon, her work was in much demand and she began traveling the country, speaking about her work and exhibiting in large folk-art shows. In 1976, she was commissioned to create a tapestry for the Bicentennial Festival of American Folklife, a work that still hangs in the Smithsonian Institute.

By the 1980s, Ethel, whom the Smithsonian had dubbed the Grandma Moses of Stitchery, no longer traveled, but she welcomed people into her home, where her pictures were hung from floor to ceiling. And lots of people came—people from all over the world. So many people, in fact, that soon it was necessary for friends and relatives to come in and serve as docents or guides.

Although her work was very popular and she could have easily made a lot of money, Ethel refused to sell any of her pictures, saying they were her memories. She discovered, however, that by donating a piece to a local charity, she was able to help out significantly with fundraising. During her later years, she ceased creating personal pieces, and only created work for charities. After a short illness, Ethel died on February 15, 1992.

Today, visitors are still welcome in Ethel's home, now the Ethel Wright Mohamed Stitchery Museum. Ethel's daughter, Carol Mohamed Ivy, is the museum's curator. As she guides visitors through the rooms, where the pictures are still hung, floor to ceiling on every wall, she offers a personal glimpse into the story behind each picture. It's a loving look into the story of a full life told with beauty and artistry.

Located at 307 Central Street.

MOVIE MUSEUMS • CANTON

Canton is the quintessential Southern town. It's so quintessential, in fact, that when Hollywood needs a Southern location, they pack up and head right on down to little ol' Canton. Commonly known as the City of Lights, say officials, Canton can now be known as the City of Lights, Camera, Action!

Tour the two Canton Film Museums, and you'll find yourself smack dab in the middle of some of your favorite movies. Here, you'll find scene recreations of movies filmed in Canton. See the café where sparks first flew between Matthew McConaughey and Sandra Bullock in *A Time to Kill*, the movie based on John Grisham's legal thriller. The law firm offices and the courthouse square, scene of the frenzied Klan march, have also been recreated.

Remember *My Dog Skip*, that sugar-sweet coming-of-age movie based on the book written by Mississippi native Willie Morris? It was filmed in Canton.

One of Canton's movie museums houses a law firm office
from *A Time to Kill*.
Courtesy of Canton CVB.

Other movies filmed in Canton and featured in the museums include *O Brother Where Art Thou?*; *The Ponder Heart*, a PBS Masterpiece Theater based on Mississippian Eudora Welty's book of the same name; *The Rising Place*; and many more. It's an interesting way to while away an afternoon.

Located at 141 North Union Street.

NATIONAL AGRICULTURAL AVIATION MUSEUM • JACKSON

Agricultural aviation? What's that? Why, it's a fancy term for crop dusting! For those of us who grew up in the rural South, it was a common sight to see a small plane dive low and drop its load of deadly chemicals over a field of crops.

It was quite a thrill back in the early days of crop dusting, when barrels of chemicals were wired to the fuselages of rickety planes. The hazards were many, from clipping the plane tail on standpipes in the field, hitting fence posts, and flying into electrical wires. On the ground, the flagman, who directed the pilot to undusted areas, faced the danger of having all those chemicals dropped on him.

Today's crop dusters are state-of-the-art machines, built for shorter takeoffs and higher spraying speeds. And instead of depending on some guy waving a white flag in the field, pilots now use high-tech GPS to tell them where to spray. But those seat-of-the-pants flyers and their

The National Agricultural Aviation Museum features exhibits chronicling the history of crop dusting.
Courtesy of Jackson CVB.

rickety planes are remembered in the National Agricultural Aviation Museum, where you'll find exhibits chronicling the history of crop dusting, including planes, equipment, and photographs. And, come prepared to spend the day, for this museum is housed within the Mississippi Agriculture and Forestry Museum that's packed with regional agricultural exhibits.

Located at 1150 Lakeland Drive.

OLD COURTHOUSE MUSEUM • VICKSBURG

Construction on Vicksburg's old courthouse began in 1858, using skilled slave artisans. Completed in 1860, the courthouse is an architectural wonder, with entrances that are flanked by four porticos, each supported by thirty-foot Ionic columns. An iron stairway ascends to the second floor courtroom, which features a cast iron judge's dias and railings. The original doors and shutters, which remain today, were also made of iron. In 1978, the American Institute of Architects chose the Old Courthouse as one of the top twenty courthouses in America.

History played out on the steps of the courthouse, with Jefferson Davis launching his political career here. Presidents Zachary Taylor, Ulysses S. Grant, William McKinley, and Theodore Roosevelt spoke from the courthouse steps. During the Civil War, Confederate Generals Stephen Lee,

The Old Courthouse as it appeared in the early 1860s.
Courtesy of the Old Courthouse Museum.

John Breckenridge, and Earl Van Dorn watched as the ironclad *Arkansas* fought its way through the federal fleet to Vicksburg. A few years later, on July 4, 1863, it was from that same cupola that Union forces raised the Stars and Stripes when Vicksburg surrendered.

When a new courthouse was built across the street, officials planned to raze the Old Courthouse, but it was saved from demolition by Vicksburg resident Eva Whitaker Davis, who convinced citizens of its historical importance. It was through her efforts that the Old Courthouse Museum was founded.

In addition to the historical significance of the building, the Old Courthouse Museum houses hundreds of exhibits containing artifacts chronicling history from pre-historic Native Americans to present day.

Located at Court Square.

JIMMY RODGERS MEMORIAL MUSEUM • MERIDIAN

Jimmie Rodgers, generally acknowledged as the Father of Country Music, was born in Meridian in 1897. He followed in his father's footsteps, working many years as a brakeman for railroads until he was forced to quit because of tuberculosis. When one door closes, another one opens, we guess.

Always interested in singing for a living, Rodgers began to pursue a career in music. He sang in vaudeville, medicine, and traveling shows. He first performed on the radio in 1927 and began recording the same year, producing songs that were different from the hillbilly and country music of the day. With his pleasing voice and music that incorporated styles of jazz and Tin Pan Alley songs, Rodgers became a quick favorite. One of his innovations was his series of songs he called Blue Yodels, which were blues songs in sound, lyrics, and style. Already known as the Singing Brakeman, he also earned the nickname America's Blue Yodler.

Rodgers's songs revolved around three themes: moving, either by horse or by train; family; and failed love. Despite suffering with tuberculosis, he kept up a smiling front and had a likeable personality that helped to make him extraordinarily popular and made him the first country music star.

His time was brief. Rodgers had been performing and recording just six years when he finally succumbed to tuberculosis. He left behind a legacy of more than one hundred recorded songs and a popularity that lives on.

Fashioned after an old railroad depot, the Jimmie Rodgers Memorial Museum celebrates the Singing Brakeman. In addition to Rodgers memorabilia, the museum features musical instruments and railroad equipment from the steam engine era.

Located on Jimmie Rodger Drive in Highland Park.

U.S.S. CAIRO • VICKSBURG

It was the morning of December 12, 1862, when the ironclad U.S.S. *Cairo* met her date with destiny. Captained by Lt. Commander Thomas Selfridge, the *Cairo* was the lead boat of a small flotilla sailing up the Yazoo River with a mission to destroy Confederate batteries and clear the channel of underwater mines. Seven miles from Vicksburg, the flotilla came under fire and Selfridge ordered his men to ready the guns. Ah, but fate is fickle and she had other plans for the *Cairo*.

On the banks of the river, two Confederate soldiers were hiding, watching the boat making its maneuver into firing position. They waited until just the right moment, and then they made their move. Suddenly the sound of two rapid explosions rent the frigid morning air. Gaping holes appeared in the ship's hull and water began flooding the lower deck. In an instant, Selfridge found himself and his crew in the drink and his ship slipping beneath the waves right in front of him. As the *Cairo* sank to the muddy bottom, she marked her place in history as the first ship to be sunk by electrically-detonated torpedoes.

The *Cairo* languished at the bottom of the Yazoo River until 1956, when a group of searchers discovered her watery grave. Recovery of cannons and other artifacts spurred interest and in 1960 the state of Mississippi began efforts to salvage the boat.

In 1964 an attempt to raise the *Cairo* intact was halted because the steel cables lifting her began cutting into the fragile timbers of the hull. Instead, the ship was cut into three sections and each section was raised individually. The sections were placed on barges and were taken to a shipyard, where the armor was removed and cleaned; the engines were disassembled, cleaned, and reassembled; and the hull was cleaned and braced. In 1977, the reconstructed hull was moved to the Vicksburg National Military Park, where it is open for viewing.

A museum adjacent to the U.S.S. *Cairo* houses artifacts recovered from the wreck site. Because of the thick layer of silt covering them, these artifacts are well preserved. The displays cover the full range of life on an ironclad, from everyday items to personal possessions of the crew members.

Located at 3201 Clay Street.

The Haunting of Mississippi

Mist rising on moonlit nights. Ghostly apparitions floating through hallowed halls. Strange and scary noises. Mississippi can be a spooky place at night. With a past so rich in history, it's no wonder there are haints wandering this land. Here's just a smattering of Mississippi's legendary ghost tales.

CEDAR GROVE MANSION INN • VICKSBURG

John Alexander Klein was a shrewd businessman. Looking forward to the day when he could afford a wife and a family, he worked hard and wisely diversified his wealth into banking, lumber, and cotton. He was a rich man by the time Elizabeth Day visited New Orleans, where Kleinman met and fell in love with her. There was one impediment to a proposal, however. Elizabeth was a mere child, much too young for marriage. Ah, but Klein was a patient man. He would bide his time and ready his life for the family he envisioned.

In 1840, Klein began construction on a Greek Revival mansion and waited patiently as Elizabeth blossomed into a woman. By 1842, Elizabeth had reached the ripe old age of sixteen and the thirty-year-old Klein thought her ready for marriage. The couple married and set off for a year-long honeymoon in Europe. In their travels, they bought lavish furnishings for their home, many of which remain today.

The Haunting of Mississippi

When the couple returned from their long honeymoon, they lived in the small cottage, until 1852, when their beautiful mansion was finally completed. They moved in and began their large family.

When the Civil War broke out, Elizabeth suffered the rejection of many of Vicksburg's elite because of family ties to General William T. Sherman. The home was bombarded by cannon fire—a cannonball remains lodged in the parlor wall—but, because it served as a Union hospital, it was spared the devastation experienced by mansions across the South.

Though they loved their beautiful home, John and Elizabeth Klein experienced much sadness here. They lost four of their ten children here. The house experienced additional sadness when a later resident, a young woman, reportedly committed suicide in the mansion's grand ballroom.

Cedar Grove, which is now operated as an elegant bed and breakfast, is said to be haunted by the spirits of its past. According to reports, the ghost of John Klein has been seen—and smelled—smoking his favorite pipe in the parlor. Elizabeth has been seen wandering the halls and stairways. There have been reports of the sound of children laughing and running through the upstairs, and sometimes there is the sound of a woman crying. In addition to the "lively" spirits of the Klein family, the spirit of the young woman who killed herself is said to appear in the ballroom on the anniversary of her death.

If you're brave enough, book a stay at the luxurious inn during the week of Halloween, when deliciously frightening candlelight tours of the mansion are conducted nightly.

Located at 220 Oak Street.

Jones County experienced hard economic times during the 1830s and 1840s. The times were so hard that many of Jones County's citizens packed up and moved on to more prosperous areas. There were so many people leaving, in fact, that the term "GTT" which meant "Gone To Texas," was widely bandied about. In time, the area became so depopulated that it was derisively called "The Free State of Jones County," a term many later mistakenly believed indicated that Jones County had set up its own republic.

COLD SPRINGS PLANTATION • PINCKNEYVILLE

Ever heard the country song *Prop Me Up Beside The Jukebox?* It's a little ditty about a guy who asks his friends to have one last party with him after he dies—to prop him up beside the jukebox and put a stiff drink in his hand. Well, that was ol' John Carmichael's last wish, as well, except that he died in the early 1800s, so there were no jukeboxes for propping.

Dr. John Carmichael, a former Army surgeon, came to Pinckneyville in 1790 to establish a plantation. Despite rooms that were lavishly furnished in the completed home, Carmichael's favorite spot in his new home was the dank and chilly wine cellar. A connoisseur, Carmichael reveled in the fine wines he collected, so much so that he moved a wooden rocking chair to the cellar and spent many a night rocking and sipping wine. He also frequently invited his friends over to enjoy his wine and to party!

So, as the story goes, Carmichael liked to party with his friends so much that he left instructions before his death that his friends were to be the ones to bury him. They were first to place his coffin in the wine cellar and then proceed to drink every drop of wine in the cellar before laying him to his final rest.

At his death, his buddies carried out his wishes, with humorous results. Seems that in consuming every last drop of the doctor's fine wine, the guys got so drunk that when they sobered up two days later, they couldn't remember just where it was they'd buried their old friend. They did finally remember several days later and the body and coffin were exhumed and taken to Woodville for a proper burial. Even then, it seems, Carmichael was not quite ready to go. On the trip to Woodville, the coffin kept falling off the wagon!

Well, the good doctor finally got buried, but it seems he's not staying put. According to reports, the unmistakable sound of a wooden rocking chair can often be heard in the Cold Spring Plantation wine cellar.

AMOS DEASON HOUSE • ELLISVILLE

When the Civil War broke out, Jones County was populated largely by poor farmers who had never owned slaves and who wanted nothing to do with the coming war. The citizens of Jones County ordered their delegate to the secession convention to vote against seceding from the Union, but the delegate got caught up in secession fervor and voted in the affirmative instead. His angry constituents hanged him in effigy and made his life so miserable that he had to leave.

One of Jones County's most vocal dissidents was a farmer named Newt Knight. He—along with many of his neighbors—refused to fight until they were drafted. Knight was serving as an orderly in a Confederate hospital when he heard about the twenty-slave legislation, a bill that exempted the wealthy who owned twenty or more slaves from fighting. Denouncing the war as "a rich man's war and a poor man's fight," he deserted and returned to Jones County, where he got together a band of like-minded fellows. Operating out of a hideout called Devil's Den in Long Leaf Swamp, the deserters reportedly conducted raids on trains headed to and from Mobile.

Knight found many of his neighbors of Jones County agreed with him and, during this time, he had as many as one hundred Confederate deserters with him, leading to rumors years later that Jones County had seceded from the Confederacy and had set up its own free republic. Many speculated this was the origin of the "Free State of Jones County," moniker, but most historians agree it never happened.

Knight's escapades soon drew attention and it wasn't long before the Confederates sent Major Amos McLemore and a contingent of soldiers to capture Knight and his band. A native of Jones County who knew the swamps as well as Knight, McLemore set up headquarters in the Amos Deason house, one of the area's few plantations. Knight was a crafty man it seems. Deciding the best defense is a good offense, he planned a peremptory strike.

It was a rainy afternoon on September 14, 1863, when Knight made his move. Bursting through the door of the

Deason home, he caught McLemore by surprise and shot him as he stood by the fireplace. McLemore reportedly gasped, "I'm killed," as he sank to the floor in a pool of blood. His dirty deed done, Knight escaped back into the swamp only to be later captured and hanged.

The Amos Deason house, built in 1840, is the oldest home in Jones County. A National Historic Landmark, it's constructed of hand-hewn heart pine, with an unusual octagon-shaped entrance. There have been so many stories of strange happenings at the Deason House that it has become a favorite on the local haunted Halloween trail.

According to reports, the stain left by the pool of McLemore's blood in front of the fireplace refused to go away, despite numerous scrubbings. The home's owners finally replaced the flooring. And that took care of that problem. Didn't stop the other thing, however. Seems that every year on September 14, the front door of the house bursts open, just as it did that rainy day so many years ago. But, no one's ever there. At least no one of flesh and blood.

Located at 410 North Deason Street.

ERROLTON • COLUMBUS

The most famous ghost of Columbus is the spirit of Nellie Weaver Tucker, whose wealthy father built an elegant mansion in 1840. The exterior of the mansion was reputed to be one of the finest designs in the city, with fluted columns, arched entries, and wide verandas. The home's interior was elegantly decorated with imported furnishings and gleaming chandeliers.

Nellie was a beautiful young woman with many friends and a huge gathering of rich suitors. Nellie's heart, however, was stolen by a common man. Maybe it was that whole man-in-uniform thing, for the object of Nellie's affections was Charles Tucker, a Columbus fireman. The couple wed in 1878, and on her wedding day, Nellie was a happy woman. To mark the momentous day, she used the diamond ring her sweetheart had given her to carve her name into a window pane of the mansion's south parlor. Hmm…maybe she was testing it to see if it was real!

Well, ol' Charles turned out to be a bit of a cad. Soon after the birth of the couple's daughter he ran off, never to be heard from again. Nellie remained in her childhood home, running a private school to support herself and her daughter. There was never enough money, and according to legend, Nellie spent her last years rocking on the porch while the elegant mansion deteriorated around her. She died in 1930.

The home sat empty and fell into great disrepair until the 1950s, when artist Erroldine Bateman bought it and began restoration. During renovations, Erroldine, who named the home Errolton, discovered the windowpane with the name NELLIE etched into it. She planned to leave the pane, but one day a ladder slipped and the pane was broken. It was replaced and no one thought anything about it until years later. By that time, Erroldine's son and his wife, Chebie, had moved into the mansion.

One sunny morning, Chebie was working in the south parlor, when a ray of bright sunlight streamed into the windows.

Chebie looked up and noticed a peculiar scratching on one of the window panes. Upon closer inspection, she found the word NELLIE etched into the same pane in the same location where the happy young bride had etched it all those years ago. No one has ever been able to explain the return of the name after the original pane was broken, but the Bateman's believe it was the spirit of Nellie voicing her approval of their renovations to her home.

Located at 216 3rd Avenue South.

The Illinois Central Light • Near Beauregard

Back in the 1920s, the Illinois Central Railroad developed a mysterious problem. It began on a dark night in 1926 at a train stop near Beauregard. As the train was nearing the stop, the engineer noticed a lantern light up ahead. As the train neared, the lantern began swinging back and forth as if someone were trying to flag him down. The engineer yelled to his brakeman and, with their eyes trained on the frantically moving light, they brought the train to a stop. The light disappeared. The engineer called out, but there was no answer. The two men disembarked and searched the area, but could find nothing.

When the train reached McComb, the men reported the incident to their supervisor, who laughed it off. He laughed it off again the next night and the next. But then, a few nights later, a different crew approached him with the same story. It was time, he decided, to brave the laughter of his superiors and report the problem.

But his superiors didn't laugh. Instead, they dispatched a couple of investigators to discover the origin of the light. Upon investigation, the detectives learned that the light occurred in the same area each time—near an old house on the outskirts of Beauregard. The house, it seems, was the home of Dr. Elias Rowan, who had built the twenty-three room house in hopes of one day turning it into a hospital.

The house was one of only three buildings to escape serious damage in the tornado of 1883, which devastated Beauregard. For a few days, the home did, indeed, serve as a hospital, as Dr. Rowan tended to the large number of citizens injured in the storm.

Dr. Rowan, the detectives learned, was a well-respected Beauregard citizen. He met his fate in 1912. Seems the good doctor was expecting a guest to come in on the Illinois Central one night. Taking up his lantern, he began walking down to the train stop. Now, by this time, the doctor was quite elderly and was hard of hearing. Many speculated that he was walking along the track and didn't hear the approaching train until it was almost upon him. When he did finally see it coming, he turned and frantically waved his lantern, but it was too late. He was struck and killed.

The detectives searched and searched, but they could find no logical explanation for the light and Illinois Central simply dropped the investigation without explanation. According to legend, the light continued to appear for many years afterward. The doctor's house stood empty for many years, with all his furnishings inside. It was finally torn down in 1940.

KING'S TAVERN • NATCHEZ

Built in the late 1700s, King's Tavern is the oldest building in Natchez. It was, in fact, the site of the town's first mail delivery, where the townspeople would gather at the tavern steps to receive their mail. The tavern was owned by Richard King, one of Natchez's most prominent citizens. He was a bit of a celebrity in town, and he and his wife enjoyed great respect.

According to legend, King hired a new serving girl named Maeline in 1789. She was a flirtatious and comely young wench. It wasn't long before the old goat began a fiery affair with young Madeline. It didn't last long, however. For, late one night King's wife caught the two in a compromising position.

King's Tavern, a popular Natchez restaurant, is haunted by a ghost named Madeline.
Courtesy of King's Tavern.

The wronged wife was furious. She wasn't about to take the betrayal lying down. The little wench was going to pay! She caught up with the young girl one evening and drove a jewel dagger into her breast. Then, as the story goes, she had her body bricked into the fireplace of the tavern's main room, tossing in the jewel dagger to do away with any evidence.

This story of murder most foul was thought to be nothing more than legend, a story concocted around the disappearance of Madeline, who may have only slunk out of town after disgracing herself with a married man. That is, until 1930, when renovations of the building uncovered a grisly find. When workers pulled down the chimney of the fireplace in the main room, they discovered the mummified remains of three bodies. An investigation revealed two of the bodies to be male. The third was that of a young girl. And next to her body was a jeweled dagger.

Was this Madeline? Had she, indeed, been brutally murdered by an enraged Mrs. King? And who were the two guys sharing her tomb? It's a mystery unsolved to this day.

Not long after the bodies were discovered strange things began happening in the tavern. Lights would flicker for no reason. Servers often noted wet footprints on the floor when there was no water around to be stepped in. There was the sound of heavy footsteps and, frequently, the chilling sound of ghostly laughter echoing through the tavern. Sometimes glasses would fly off the shelves and many guests reported feeling a sudden tightness in their necks and shoulders, accompanied by a feeling of heaviness in their chests.

In 2000, a local television station, spurred by reports of ghostly happenings, decided to conduct an investigation. They weren't disappointed. During the long, dark night, investigators saw moving shadows—shadows for which there was no source. Cameras malfunctioned for no reason and, in one of the bedrooms—a room that was empty—the voice of a woman was recorded.

Perhaps the most significant event occurred in another bedroom, where one of the investigators had gone for a short nap. The reporter had been inside the room for only a few minutes when she was startled by the sound of an alarm. It was the alarm on a temperature sensor, a device used by paranormal investigators. As she watched the gauge, the temperature in the room suddenly dropped twenty-three degrees. To investigators, a sudden temperature drop signals the presence of otherworldly entities.

Today, King's Tavern is a popular Natchez restaurant, serving up fine steak, seafood, and drinks. And, for desert, you can pop up to the third floor bedrooms for a deliciously scary search for Madeline.

Located at 619 Jefferson Street.

LINDEN HOUSE • NATCHEZ

Sitting regally atop a gentle slope amid moss-laden oaks, Linden House evokes images of the grand old South, with hoop-skirted ladies sweeping down curving stairways and elegantly dressed gentlemen arriving on majestic steeds. Stepping in the front door, you'll feel as if you're entering Tara. Well, OK, there's a good reason for that. The front door of Linden was copied for Tara in the movie *Gone With The Wind*.

Linden was built in 1790 and was the home of Thomas B.

Reed, the first elected U.S. Senator from Mississippi. A Federal architecture gem, it has been occupied by the Conner family for six generations. The Richard Conner Feltus family now operates the home as a bed and breakfast, with luxuriously-appointed rooms, furnished with family antiques and high-canopied beds. Each room opens onto a gallery, where old-fashioned rocking chairs invite you out to sit a spell.

Any home with this much history is bound to have a spirit or two lurking about. At Linden, guests have reported hearing the sound of a horse-drawn buggy pulling into the front driveway and the sound of a cane tapping has been heard in the west gallery. There have also been ghost sightings here. A man in a top hat has been seen many times in the window of the children's room. The most frightening apparition, however, is that of a woman. She's often sighted on the roof of the east wing. As you watch, she takes a flying leap off the edge of the roof, but disappears before she hits the ground.

Located at 1 Linden Place.

Well, here's a really weird happening. On May 11, 1887, during a violent hailstorm near Bovina, it started rainin' turtles. Well, a turtle, anyway. According to records, a six-inch by eight-inch gopher turtle hurtled to the ground and hit with a resounding smack. Poor little thing was frozen solid. Since everyone knows that turtles can't fly, it makes you wonder how he got up there.

The Haunting of Mississippi

MONMOUTH PLANTATION • NATCHEZ

Built in 1818, this beautiful two-story Federal-style mansion was bought by General John Quitman for $12,000 in 1826. Quitman, a Yankee by birth, had moved South and made his fortune in Mississippi. He was practicing law in Natchez when he bought Monmouth for his wife, just after the birth of their first child. A hero of the Mexican War, Quitman moved into politics, serving as one of Mississippi's first governors and later as a state senator.

As a transplanted Southerner, Quitman embraced the Southern way of life, and argued vehemently in Congress that the South be allowed to secede. Not long after making that argument, Quitman and numerous fellow secessionists became very ill. Many died of the mysterious illness, and although Quitman held on for two years, it's believed it was this illness that killed him. Theories abound that Quitman and the other Southerners were poisoned by abolitionists.

Although Quitman died before the Civil War began, his vociferous defense of secession was remembered by the Union. During the war, Monmouth was treated roughly by Union soldiers, but was saved from total destruction by Quitman's daughters, who pledged allegiance to the Union to keep the soldiers from burning their home.

Monmouth stayed in the Quitman family until 1914, when Rose, the last daughter, passed away. A series of owners passed through Monmouth, but the place was much neglected and had fallen to great disrepair when the present owners bought it and began renovating the home to operate as a bed and breakfast.

It was during these renovations that the spirit of John Quitman began to appear, perhaps to check out what the new owners were planning for his home. The first indication of his return was the strong uneasy feeling the workers felt anytime they were inside the house. Next, the sound of heavy footsteps was heard by numerous people, from the owners to the workers, and even the police.

Monmouth Plantation is haunted by its former owner, John Quitman.
Courtesy of Mississippi Development Authority/Division of Tourism.

Once renovations were complete and the bed and breakfast opened, it's reported that Quitman often would make late-night visits to rooms to check up on the guests. On one particular occasion, a gentleman staying in Room 30 was awakened by a strange clinking sound. Unable to go back to sleep, he got up and sat in a wicker rocker on the porch. As he sat, he continued to hear the sound. Suddenly he saw a man approaching. The man was wearing a blue uniform (Quitman, remember, was a Mexican War hero), with a cloud of dust seeming to swirl from his shoulders. It was the man's spurs, the guest realized, that were making the peculiar clinking sound. He stood to greet the man only to see him disappear before his eyes. In a tour the next day, he was shown a portrait of Quitman and immediately recognized his late-night visitor.

According to reports, Quitman continues to check in on guests every now and again, adding a wonderful thrill to a stay at this magnificent inn.

Located at 36 Melrose Avenue.

TEMPLE HEIGHTS • COLUMBUS

Temple Heights was a grand Federal-style mansion built in 1837 by General Richard Brownrigg, whose successful Columbus business made it necessary for him to move his family in from their plantation five miles away. Financial ruin necessitated the sale of the house only a few years later.

The house changed hands several times before its sale to the Reverend J.H. Kennebrew, a retired Methodist minister with five daughters. Kennebrew specified in his will that the house not be sold until all his daughters—Daisy, Laura, Jessie, Ruth, and Elizabeth—were married off and had another place to live. Well, as fate would have it, only two of the girls found husbands. The other three remained at Temple Heights their entire lives.

By most accounts, all the girls were a bit eccentric, but the most eccentric by far was the youngest, Miss Elizabeth. According to legend, ol' Lizzie was quite a sight and a bit of a fright. She powdered her face with chalk dust and painted her cheeks and lips with Mercurochrome. To top it all off, Elizabeth dyed her hair a garish shade of red. It was as if she'd stepped right out of a Tennessee Williams play!

As the youngest, Elizabeth was the last to pass on. She lived at Temple Heights until her death in 1965. The Butlers, the present owners, bought the house in 1967 and restored it to its former glory. From the moment they moved in, the Butlers say they knew they weren't alone. They were often startled by unexplained noises, such as the sudden sounds of objects crashing to the floor or breaking glass. A search of the house could turn up nothing broken or out of place. At other times, they heard the sound of murmuring voices echoing through the hallways and in empty rooms.

In an effort to discover with whom they were sharing their home, the Butlers searched the history of the house. Since Miss Elizabeth was the last occupant, they decided she had to be the one. Time slipped by and the family grew accustomed to the strange noises and occurrences, but it was years before their suspicion about the identity of their resident ghost was confirmed.

By that time, the home had been restored, and the Butlers became well-known for their preservation efforts. Listed on the National Registry of Historic Places, Temple Heights was a popular stop on the Columbus Pilgrimage Tour, a tour of antebellum homes. One afternoon, a tour guide passing the Butler's bedroom caught sight of a ghostly figure standing in the middle of the room. She rushed downstairs and described the apparition to the group. "Why you've just described Elizabeth Kennebrew perfectly," said an older woman, who was a long-time Columbus resident and an acquaintance of the eccentric old lady.

Temple Heights remains a favorite tour site, open three days a week or by appointment. Be prepared, though, for Miss Elizabeth is still haunting the place and tour participants have reported many strange events!

Located at 515 Ninth Street North.

Eat, Drink, and Be Merry!

Eating out in Strange But True Mississippi is more than a meal. It's an experience. There are restaurants and bars galore along the back roads trail, some historic, some haunted, some just plain fun.

AUNT JENNY'S CATFISH • OCEAN SPRINGS

True to its name, Aunt Jenny's offers pond fresh catfish, fried light, just like your mama used to cook it. It's served up with country seasoned hushpuppies, baked yams, cole slaw, and good ol' homemade biscuits and jelly. 'Course that's not all Aunt Jenny serves. She's also got crispy fried chicken and shrimp and a smattering of Creole dishes. It's good food, for sure. But that's not the only reason this restaurant is included on our tour. You see, Aunt Jenny's is home to a few otherwordly entities.

It's no surprise that a few spirits are hanging out here. The restaurant is housed in an 1852 antebellum mansion nestled beneath five-hundred-year-old oaks. Oooo, better yet, it once served as an asylum! Reportedly there have been many incidents suggesting that some of the inmates are still around.

Some of these incidents have occurred in the Julep Room Lounge, a place where Elvis Presley is reputed to have frequented when he was alive and kicking. According to employee reports, the juke box in the Julep Room has been known to start playing, despite the fact that it's unplugged at the time. When this happens, it plays ragtime songs, which are not in the jukebox!

In addition, customers often have offered to buy a drink for that man at the end of the bar—the one wearing black pants and a white shirt. What? But he was right there! He had dark hair! I saw him! Other times employees have reported seeing movement out of the corners of their eyes when no one was there, faucets that turn on by themselves, and light bulbs being unscrewed.

Located at 1217 Washington Avenue.

ANTIQUE MALL AND CROWN RESTAURANT • INDIANOLA

Well, y'all, the middle of a Mississippi cotton field is the last place you'd expect to be served high tea, but, hey, there it is! The Crown Restaurant was opened in 1972—out in the middle of an Indianola cotton field—as a sideline to Tony and Evelyn Roughton's antique sales business. Looking for a way to bring in more customers, Evelyn, who'd developed a love for all things British while living in England, came up with the high tea idea. She began serving lunch and afternoon tea in an English pub setting, using antique tables and chairs.

You wouldn't think such a thing would go over in little rural Indianola. Shows how much we know. But soon folks were making the trip out to the country just for lunch, and the antique business became the sideline.

In 1996, the Crown Restaurant moved into Indianola, where Evelyn loves to experiment with new and different dishes, including those with catfish, an important Mississippi industry. The restaurant has been featured on the Food Network, Turner South,

A server at the Crown Restaurant presents their famous Bayou Beer Bread.
Courtesy of the Crown Restaurant.

and CNN and in *Southern Living* Magazine.

BETTY DAVIS GROCERY • WATERFORD

Betty Davis (no relation to the movie star) Grocery is just what it says—a convenience grocery located out on Highway 7, with only a Budweiser sign heralding its existence. But there's one thing setting Betty's apart from other convenience stores: They serve up some mean barbecue. You won't find fancy food here. Nor any fancy places to sit. There's just one picnic table in the joint. If it's crowded, and it probably will be, just take your food outside beneath the spreading shade trees. Enjoy a little nature while you chew on an order of smoky ribs slathered in tangy red sauce. You'll find yourself wanting to suck the marrow right out of 'em!

Located 3359 Old Oxford Road.

> U.S Highway 90 between Bay St. Louis, Mississippi, and New Orleans, Louisiana, is known as the Praline Capital of the World. By the way: That's pronounced praw-leen.

BIG APPLE INN • JACKSON

OK, we gotta admit it. Nothing on God's green earth can make us eat a pig's ear sandwich. But we'd be remiss in our Strange But True tour if we didn't tell you about the little ol' restaurant that's famous for such a delicacy.

The Big Apple Inn, named for a big dance that used to be held in Jackson, got its start when Gene Lee Sr. began selling tamales from a bucket on the street corner in the 1930s. In 1939, he opened the small restaurant on Farish Street, where he's been serving up good food ever since.

The pig's ear sandwich came about when the local butcher asked Lee if he could use the pig's ears he had left over in his shop. Not one to turn down a bargain, Lee took 'em and began experimentin' with 'em. He'd boil 'em up with different spices and try them out. Finally hitting upon just the right combination, he slapped 'em between two pieces of bread, and voilà! A new delicacy was born.

Now, we can't tell you from experience, but from what we hear, pig's ear sandwiches taste like a cross between ham and roast beef. The meat consistency is like bologna. As far as spicy goes—you can order it anywhere from mild to hot.

OK, we've told you about it. Now we gotta worry about all those little pigs running around with no ears.

Located at 509 North Farish Street.

BLOW FLY INN • GULFPORT

According to restaurant legend, the Blow Fly Inn got its name because back forty years ago folks kept asking owner Albert Malone where his restaurant, then known as Hickory's Bar-B-Que, was. His answer? "Go to Pass Road, take a right, and follow the string of blow flies." Not a ringing endorsement, we'd say, but the food was good and the place was soon being called the Blow Fly Inn by local wags. When Malone officially changed the name, the phone company refused him a listing, saying the name was inappropriate. That is, until they had so many information requests for the restaurant that they finally gave in.

The Blow Fly Inn is famous for its Gulf Coast seafood. In addition, you'll find steaks, prime rib, barbecue, and pasta dishes. Oh, and don't worry 'bout those blow flies on your plate. They're just made of plastic.

Hurricane Katrina devastated this small coastal town and destroyed a huge number of local landmarks. The building that housed the historic Blow Fly Inn was, alas, one of those casualties. But buildings can be rebuilt and Katrina in no way damaged the spirits of those who weathered her wrath. At the time of publication, the Blow Fly Inn had been relocated to the

Airport Holiday Inn until the building at Bayou Bernard can be rebuilt.

Located at 9415 Highway 49.

THE BLUE & WHITE RESTAURANT • TUNICA

Even in the Deep South these days it's sometimes hard to find a good ol' Southern restaurant with mama's good cookin'. But, that's just what you find at the Blue & White. Since 1937, they've been serving up the best of Southern cuisine, food so good it makes you think of Gramma and those huge Sunday dinners she used to slave over.

Hit the lunch buffet and you've got some hard decisions to make. What will it be today? Fried chicken? Meatloaf? No, wait, the chicken and melt-in-your-mouth dumplin's! Don't forget to get one of the cat head biscuits and banana puddin' for dessert. Bring on the sweet tea, and we've been transported to a higher plane.

In a town that's rife with casinos and the fare that's gobbled down between bouts of gambling away your life savings, the Blue and White stands as testimony to the days when Tunica was just a sleepy Mississippi burg. It's a beautiful sight out there on Highway 61, all bright white with its electric blue roof and trademark blue sign. You can't miss it, and believe us, you don't want to.

Located at 1355 U.S. Highway 61 North.

DÉJÀ VU • RIDGELAND

They musta named it this because as soon as you leave you wanna do it all over again. The fare at Déjà Vu is the best Cajun cooking you'll find this side of New Orleans. Their jambalaya, spicy andouille sausage, and shrimp and chicken gumbo are famous in these parts. The patio, serviced by a full bar, is a favorite after-work hangout.

Located at 810 Lake Harbor Drive.

> Premier Playboy Hugh Hefner has stated that the most beautiful women in the world come from Oxford and the surrounding area.

DOE'S EAT PLACE • GREENVILLE

According to many food critics, Doe's serves the best steaks in America. Opened in a predominately African-American neighborhood in 1941, Doe's began life as a honky-tonk, serving such items as buffalo wings, fish, and chili. The honky-tonk was for blacks only; others were required to go around back. Not long after the business opened, a local doctor began coming 'round to the back for a meal between house calls (they used to do that, you know). Doe would cook him up a steak on the grill and it wasn't long before the doc brought along another doc and that doc brought a lawyer. Soon, Doe found he had a bigger business going in the back. Calling in wife, Mamie, who contributed her special recipe for tamales, and his in-laws, Doe closed the honky-tonk and moved the eating place out front, where he and Mamie gained a reputation for serving up good food.

Doe and Mamie are gone now, but the restaurant is still family-run, taken over by their sons in the 1970s. The boys haven't done much in the way of building upkeep. Located in a questionable part of town, it's dilapidated, with sloping floors and a sign that's seen better days. You enter through the kitchen and find a table in the small dining room, where none of the tablecloths or silverware matches. Some of the tables are even located in the kitchen, spread among the work stations, where servers make the salads and prepare side orders. True, there are now Doe's restaurants in several Mississippi towns, but this is a part of history. I mean, really, where else can you eat your upscale cut of beef beneath an ancient stuffed—pheasant?—that's loosing its stuffing?

Who needs ambience when the food is this good? Steaks are the specialty. Sold by the pound, they're cut fresh daily from whole beef loins. Foodies everywhere sing their praises.

Located at 502 Nelson Street.

In 1898, Edward Charles Edmond Barq made soft drink history in Biloxi by bottling a unique root beer formula. Barq added more carbonation to his concoction and cut the amount of sugar, which resulted in a root beer with more "bite" than other formulas. Barq's was wildly popular and by 1937, there were more than sixty-two bottling plants in twenty-two states producing Barq's. Today, advertising under the slogan "Barq's has bite," Barq's is the country's most popular root beer.

FAT MAMA'S TAMALES • NATCHEZ

Fat Mama's is home of the world famous Knock You Naked Margarita! Be extra careful with these industrial strength libations, else you'll find yourself waking up with a head the size of a mush melon and vague memories of dancing a tabletop two-step wearing nothing but your boots and a smile.

One way to avoid losing all your inhibitions is to eat a little something with those margaritas. Fat Mama's offers a mix of Mexican fare—hot tamales, chili, gringo pies, gringo casseroles, to name just a few. There's even Cajun Boudin on the menu!

Fat Mama's Tamales offers a variety of Mexican fare.
Courtesy of Fat Mama's Tamales.

Now don't you go off without your Knock You Naked at Fat Mama's T-shirt. For a mere twenty-five buckaroos, you, too, can have a garment that will bring back hazy memories of table top dances.

Located at 500 South Canal Street.

Eat, Drink, and Be Merry!

GROUND ZERO BLUES CLUB • CLARKSDALE

Located inside an old cotton warehouse, this get-down serious blues club has earned quite a reputation since its 2001 opening. The club, co-owned by Academy award-winning actor Morgan Freeman, features primarily Delta Blues musicians, who carry on in the musical footsteps of their forefathers.

Stepping through the door of Ground Zero is like stepping through a time portal. The sweaty blues beat wraps itself around you as you trod the wooden floors, past the up-front pool tables, to the graffiti-covered bar. Christmas lights and beer signs provide dim illumination, while garland and found objects, such as an old saxophone, hang from exposed ceiling pipes. T-shirts, photographs, and graffiti cover the brick walls.

In addition to good music and good food, Ground Zero offers accommodations in several loft apartments. Retro-decorated, these spacious rooms allow you to extend your experience past the time when you can no longer keep your eyes open. You can drift off to sleep to the blues lullaby winding its way up from the bar downstairs.

Freeman is a resident of the Clarksdale area and when he's not off in some exotic location filming a movie, he makes frequent appearances at Ground Zero. If you're lucky, you might find him out jukin' on the dance floor. May even have some of his Hollywood buds with him. But even if he's not there, the blues and good food are worth the trip.

Located at 0 Blues Alley.

Got milk? Mississippi does. In 1984, the Mississippi State Legislature adopted milk as the state beverage. In 2001, Mississippi had three Grade A diary processing plants and 365 Grade A dairy farms. These farms produced 57,790,698 gallons of milk in 2001.

LUSCO'S • GREENWOOD

Dining at Lusco's takes you back to the days of Prohibition. The restaurant got its start back in the 1920s, when Charles "Papa" Lusco delivered supplies on his horse-drawn wagon to local cotton planters. When the planters came into town, they stopped in at the Luscos' market, where Mama Lusco served up plates of her spaghetti in the back. By 1933, Papa had constructed secret rooms in the back and, in order to sneak the cotton planters a little taste of his homemade wine to go with their spaghetti, he hung curtains around each room.

Of course, Prohibition ended in the thirties, but according to local gossip, the wealthy cotton planters liked the privacy offered by the curtains, behind which they would "entertain" their mistresses. Since you never knew what might be going on behind those curtains, buzzers were used to signal that it was safe to enter.

Today, Lusco's is well-known for its upscale cuisine, a fusion of Italian, Southern, and Creole cooking.

As a bonus, you'll get to dine in complete privacy behind those famed curtains, where you summon your server with a buzzer. Just remember to behave yourself. The management frowns on hanky-panky these days.

Located at 722 Carrollton Avenue.

Mammy's Cupboard • Natchez

Built in 1940, Mammy's Cupboard was originally a gas station, an architectural oddity designed to lure folks in. She truly was politically incorrect back then, a huge slave-type mammy, complete with kerchief covered head and voluminous brick skirts, which comprised the building. She's weathered the years, serving variously as a gas station, a gift shop, and, several times, as a restaurant.

Today, her political incorrectness has been muted. Painted a lighter shade of pale, she sports enough rouge to make her the envy of any Southern nursing home. Her pink polka dot kerchief matches the garish pink of her skirts. And, inside those pink-brick skirts, you'll find down home cookin' just like your mammy used to make.

Located at 555 Highway 61 North.

The Old Country Store • Lorman

If you grew up in the South, you know about the old country store. It was the place you went to sell cotton and other farm products and to buy your household supplies. From coffee to overalls, you could find whatever you needed stacked on shelves and piled into bins inside the huge wooden structures.

Built in 1875, the Old Country Store in Lorman served as a commerce center for rural Jefferson County for more than one hundred years. Today, it looks just as it did back then. Operated as a popular down-home cooking restaurant, the large wooden building has been preserved, but not restored. Its exterior walls are weathered and unpainted, adorned by rusting Pepsi signs. The red tin roof is faded and the front porch railing is missing a number of spindles. It's a visit back to a simpler time.

Located at 18801 U.S. Highway 61.

PEGGY'S • PHILADELPHIA

Only in the South! In 1961, Peggy Webb needed to make some money. But she also needed to stay home and raise her three kids. Being an excellent cook, she began making home cooked meals for the working folks. Blocking off the hallway of her home, she placed a long buffet along the wall and filled it with Southern dishes. Folks would come in, help themselves to the food, pour themselves some good ol' sweet tea, and seat themselves at one of the tables placed around the dining room of Peggy's home. When they finished, they'd drop their money into a basket and leave.

Well, word spread about Peggy's good cooking and soon her little business became the family's major source of income, run by Peggy and husband, Don. In 2002, Peggy and Don turned the business over to their youngest, Stan, who has continued the family tradition of good food and trust in people.

Dining at Peggy's is much as it was in those first days. You enter the 1950s home, where you'll find the hallway blocked off and a long buffet covered with all sorts of Southern dishes. Help yourself to the food. Pour yourself some sweet tea. And, seat yourself at one of the large tables, where you'll make new friends as you rave over the food. When you've finished, don't bother looking for the cash register. There's not one. Just drop your money in the basket on the way out. We trust you.

Located at 512 Bay Street East.

PHILLIP'S GROCERY • HOLLY SPRINGS

Ooo la la! This old building has quite the checkered past! Built in 1882, it once served as a speakeasy and a brothel. It looks the part, too. You can well imagine gaudy ladies of the evening leaning over the weathered upstairs balcony and calling down to the "gentlemen" as they entered the downstairs saloon.

In 1919, the building became a grocery store and by the 1940s, began building a reputation for its juicy All-American hamburgers. That reputation culminated in 1989, with national acclaim, when *USA Today* named Phillip's Grocery's burger to the Top 3 in the nation. Today, folks come from around the country for Phillip's burgers, served simply in a brown bag and wrapped in yellow wax paper. You can get it to go or eat in at a variety of eclectic seating, including stools at a short counter, a smattering of old school desks, or a few odd tables. Outside, you'll find a couple of picnic tables with a view of the old railroad depot. Yeah, we know. It's not fancy. But who cares when the burgers are this good?

Located at 541A East Van Dorn Avenue.

Funny Happenings Here

Eggs falling from the sky. Rooster crowings and cow mooings. Hootnannies and pointed toe dances. There are weird things going on in Strange But True Mississippi.

BLUEBERRY JUBILEE • POPLARVILLE

Did you know that the blueberry not only tastes good, but it's good for you, too? It's true! Blueberries contain no fat and no cholesterol, and they're low in calories. They are a good source of Vitamin C and fiber, and they have powerful antioxidant properties, which means they help fight aging, cancer, and heart disease.

Poplarville and Pearl River County, indeed, all of Mississippi, have another good reason for feting the blueberry with an annual jubilee. You see, Mississippi blueberry growers, many of whom are located in the Poplarville area, produce more than 9.6 million pounds of blueberries annually, which results in an economic impact of $12.32 million annually. Good reason to celebrate, eh?

And celebrate they do. Things kick off with a beauty pageant. There're special events, such as a 5K run, storytelling by the Poplarville Storytelling Guild, tours of local blueberry farms, and a baby crawl. And, there's plenty of live entertainment, including music and dancing, lots of food, and arts and crafts for sale. A special treat is the storytelling workshop, presented by the Poplarville Storytelling Guild. It's a berry, berry good time!

Held annually in June.

CHEF POULE FESTIVAL • TYLERTOWN

Poule. It's French for chicken, y'all. You can guess which industry is important to Tylertown's economy. This day-long eggstravaganza is a scramble of poultry-themed events. There's a series of pageants for beauties of all ages—from Little Miss Chick all the way to Old Biddy. A lot of eggs get broken in the kid's egg relay, and there's lots of crowing going on in the rooster crowing contest. Live entertainment includes puppet shows and country, gospel, and bluegrass music. The day's highlight is the cook-off, where local chefs vie for the title of Chef Poule and the opportunity to crow about their success for the whole year. It's a cackling good time you won't want to miss.

Held annually on the last Saturday in September.

CHOCTAW INDIAN FAIR • PHILADELPHIA

There are several legends concerning the origins of the Choctaw tribe. According to one legend, the entire tribe sprang, fully-formed, from beneath the earth at Nanih Waiya. In another legend, the Choctaw originated in the land of mountains of snow, west of the great river. They were led eastward by a great medicine man, who would drive a red stick into the ground every night. Each morning, they would find the stick leaning eastward, a sign, the medicine man said, that they should continue in that direction. Finally one morning, they awoke to find the stick remaining upright. This, they knew, was where the Great Spirit wanted them to live. They named the place Nanih Waiya, which means "leaning hill."

Those lyrical legends, say archeologists, exist to explain the sudden origins of the Choctaw tribe, which, according to their research, did not exist as a tribe until the seventeenth century. The tribe, they say, was formed by a coalescence of the remnants of several southeastern tribes, a coalescence that occurred in the area known as Nanih Waiya.

Located in Neshoba County, the lands of Nanih Waiya were taken by the state and, at one point, were designated as a state park. These lands, however, have since been returned to Mississippi's Choctaw tribe. Whatever the true origins of the Choctaw, there's no doubt that Nanih Waiya and the surrounding area is sacred land and is considered the homeland of the tribe.

For almost sixty years, the Choctaw tribe has held an annual fair on their tribal lands. This fair is based on the custom of the New Corn Ceremony, when neighboring tribes would gather at harvest time to celebrate their bounties and pay homage to their traditions. Starting as a secular celebration, the Choctaw Indian Fair has emerged as an opportunity for the tribe to open the reservation and share its way of life with visitors. Four jam-packed days, the fair has evolved into an amalgam of traditional Choctaw ceremonies and activities and mainstream entertainment.

Funny Happenings Here

Dairy Festival • Tylertown

Walthall County bills itself as the Cream Pitcher of Mississippi. There's a reason for that. You see, back in the day, the area was filled with cotton farmers accustomed to plowing their fields with mules and picking their crops by hand. But then the fifties rolled around and farming became mechanized, with big pieces of equipment that cost a fortune. Unable to afford the equipment necessary to stay competitive, Walthall's farmers decided they needed a new way to make a living. Something that didn't require lots of fancy equipment. Something there was a big market for.

Well, New Orleans was relatively close. And those folks were in need of lots of fresh milk. A few cows—a lot less expensive than cotton machinery—and some milking equipment and they were in business. By the 1970s, there were four hundred dairy farms operating in the county. As time passed, of course, things changed. The larger farms bought out the smaller. Today the county has sixty-two Grade A dairy farms, which supply $16 million in revenue for the county.

The tradition of Tylertown's Dairy Festival began more than thirty years ago as a way for local Dairymen to express their gratitude to their community. It's the oldest and biggest one-day event in the county. Every year, thousands gather for the non-stop activities. There is, of course, a Dairy Festival Queen pageant. There also are such activities as a mooing contest, a butter churning contest, baby contests, sack races, and the World Famous Turtle Races. OK, that one's a little slow. But it's lots of fun. There's also plenty of good food and live entertainment. The day concludes with a gospel singing under the trees, capped by a spectacular fireworks display.

Held annually the first Saturday in June.

EASTER EGG DROP • PICAYUNE

Eggs away! Why hunt for Easter eggs when you can drop 'em out of airplanes like little atomic bombs? And all for a good cause or three. The Picayune Easter Egg Drop is an annual event residents can participate in by purchasing a plastic raffle egg, the proceeds of which go to community needs. The eggs—up to four thousand of 'em—containing raffle tickets, are loaded onto vintage airplanes and are dropped over designated target areas. Those holding winning tickets win money and other prizes. In addition to the egg drop, the event features such activities as pony rides, hot air balloon rides, arts and crafts, and face painting.

Held in April.

ELVIS FESTIVAL • TUPELO

As the birthplace of the King, Tupelo is aware of its responsibility to keep the legend alive. And so, every year they throw a big festival in his honor.

The celebration revisits the day in 1956 when the hometown boy came home for the first time to perform as a star. There's a re-creation of Elvis's homecoming parade, held that day in 1956, followed by a weekend of fun Elvis activities.

Think you do a pretty good Elvis impersonation? Cool, man! Get up there on stage and let's see. One of the newest events of the festival is the Tribute Artist Competition. Contestants don their jumpsuits and hit the stage at the Tupelo fairgrounds— where Elvis performed in 1956—and see if they can out-gyrate the other contestants. The winner will represent Tupelo in the Ultimate Elvis Tribute Competition in Memphis.

A local man woos the crowd during the Tribute Artist Competition. Courtesy of Tupelo CVB.

There are, of course, live performances all weekend, all Elvis all the time. There're also other activities, such as the Running with the King 5K Run, the Walk a Mile in My Shoes (blue suede, we bet) charity walk, and the Elvis Recliner Races. Think your hound dog bears a close resemblance to the King? Well, dress him up in his bejeweled cape and sunglasses and come on down for the Elvis Lookalike Pet Parade! Oh! And if you just can't stand the heartbreak of staying in a hotel, fear not. You can camp out at one of the area's many camp grounds. The Elvis Presley Campground would be most appropriate, we think.

Held annually in June.

Because of an unusual state law requiring casinos to be located on the water, the flamboyant casinos of Biloxi and Gulfport were built on barges on the water, many of which were engineered to rise and fall with the tides. When Hurricane Katrina blew through, she devastated the area's "Casino Row." Many of the casinos have already been rebuilt and others will open soon. Though still flamboyant, the buildings have their uniqueness. To hasten rebuilding, Mississippi changed the law, now allowing casinos to be built on land.

FALL MUSTER • GULFPORT

Civil War re-enactments are popular events around the South. Maybe we think if we keep re-doing it, we'll finally chase those Yankees back over the Mason-Dixon line. More likely, it's just a good excuse to dress up in old clothes and play soldier.

During the annual Fall Muster, the sights, sounds, and smells of the Civil War are relived with cavalry, infantry, and cannon demonstrations. Soldiers in authentic Union and Confederate uniforms battle it out all over again in daily skirmishes. In addition to these daily battles, there are authentic encampments, where visitors learn how soldiers lived during these times.

The Fall Muster traditionally takes place on the grounds of Beauvoir, a historic mansion in Gulfport. Beauvoir was badly damaged by Hurricane Katrina and the Fall Muster has been temporarily relocated to Harrison County Fairgrounds. All proceeds from the Fall Muster are going toward rebuilding the mansion, with a projected completion date in 2008.

Held annually in October.

FIDDLIN' WITH THE FROGS FESTIVAL • GRENADA

Well, no, you won't find no fiddlin' frogs here, but that won't matter, 'cause the folks that are fiddlin' will have you hoppin' with pleasure. This bluegrass festival, held at Frog Hollow Campgrounds, features live entertainment, arts and crafts, and plenty of food. This is a family event, so leave the bourbon at home and watch yore mouth. They don't allow drinkin' or cussin'!

Confederate General Nathan Bedford Forrest was reared in Benton County. Military historians acclaim him as the foremost cavalry officer the country has ever known.

GEORGE OHR FESTIVAL OF ARTS • BILOXI

Calling himself "The Mad Potter," George Ohr fashioned himself an eccentric persona as a brash, mischievous imp with flowing hair and beard. His moustache was so long he often hooked it around his ears. He was born in Biloxi in 1857, and, although today he is known as the country's first art potter, his talent went unrecognized in his lifetime.

After learning the potter craft in New Orleans, Ohr

returned to Biloxi and built his own shop from the bottom up, constructing the building and making his own kiln and potter's wheel. He rowed a skiff on the Tchoutacabouffa River and dug his own clay. He made practical pieces, but also found time to fashion finer, never-before-seen works. These delicate, thin-walled pieces caught the attention of the art world, but did not gain popularity with the public, who refused to pay the exorbitant prices Ohr demanded.

Supremely confident in his talent, Ohr refused to come down on his prices and after his death in 1918, six thousand pieces were crated up and stored in his building, which his sons turned into an auto repair shop. The cache was discovered in 1968 by an antique dealer, who paid the Ohr family $50,000 for them and began circulating them in the art world. The Mad Potter's faith in his talent has finally been vindicated. Today, a George Ohr piece sells for thousands of dollars, much more than even Ohr envisioned.

The George Ohr Fall Festival of Arts showcases the artwork of more than eighty local and Southeastern artists. Visitors can find unique paintings, jewelry, photography, and pottery. Live demonstrations give an inside look at the artists at work. In addition, you can tap into your own muse with hands-on activities.

THE GREAT DELTA BEAR AFFAIR • ROLLING FORK

Did you know that the Teddy Bear got its start in Mississippi? It's true! Back in 1902, then-President Theodore Roosevelt came to the state to settle a border dispute with

Louisiana. During his spare time, the president indulged in a little bear hunting near Onward. Unfortunately, the bears did not cooperate and the hunt was fruitless. Not wanting the president of the United States to go home empty handed, the hunting party brought a bear to the camp for him to shoot. But as President Teddy drew a bead on the hapless ursine, he saw that it was exhausted. Taking a closer look, he found it to be small, possibly just a cub, and it had a hurt foot. The President lowered his gun and

A Teddy Roosevelt impersonator makes special appearances during the Great Delta Bear Affair.
Courtesy of the Great Delta Bear Affair.

refused to shoot the poor thing, saying it was unsporting. Bully!

When the news of the President's compassion reached the ears of New York merchant Morris Michton, it sparked an inspiration. Michton created a cuddly stuffed toy bear he called "Teddy's Bear," and placed it in the window of his candy store. The bear's popularity was so great that it led to the formation of the Ideal Toy Corporation in 1903. It's still one of the most popular toys.

In 2002, the one hundredth anniversary of the great bear hunt, the community of Rolling Fork held the first Great Delta Bear Affair. Designed to raise wildlife awareness, the celebration includes wildlife education, archeological and birding tours, musical acts, storytelling, book signings, and an interactive educational area. One of the celebration highlights is an appearance by Case Hicks, famed Teddy Roosevelt impersonator.

Held in October.

THE GREAT MISSISSIPPI RIVER BALLOON RACE • NATCHEZ

Well, here's a high flying celebration. The Great Mississippi River Balloon Race, voted Mississippi's Best Annual Event by readers of *Mississippi Magazine*, features high-flying hot air balloons in exciting races over the picturesque Mississippi landscape. At any given moment, the sky may be filled with as

The Great Mississippi River Balloon Race was once voted Mississippi's Best Annual Event.
Courtesy of Mississippi Development Authority/Division of Tourism.

many as one hundred brightly-colored balloons. In addition to the balloon races, the weekend is filled with live entertainment performed by a variety of local bands.

Held annually in October.

> The Mississippi River has many nicknames. It's known variously as the Mighty Mississippi, the Big Muddy, Old Man River, the Father of Waters, and the Great River.

HIGHWAY 61 BLUES FESTIVAL • LELAND

U.S. Route 61, a 1,400-mile stretch from Minnesota to New Orleans, runs right through the heart of the Mississippi Delta. It's along this stretch of highway that legendary musicians created a new sound that became known as the blues. Robert Johnson, Son House, Charley Patton, Howlin' Wolf, legends all, got their starts playing juke joints and barn dances along Highway 61.

The famed "Crossroads," where Robert

A performer at the Highway 61 Blues Festival teaches children how to dance.
Courtesy of Highway 61 Blues Museum.

Johnson is reputed to have sold his soul in return for his mastery of the blues, is located here. Mississippians Muddy Water and Bo Diddley took the blues up the highway to Chicago. No doubt about it, U.S. Route 61 is the Blues Highway.

The Highway 61 Blues Festival honors the memory of these great musicians and celebrates their music by bringing today's hottest blues players to the stage. Featured musicians include acts such as Willie Foster, T-Model Ford, Eddie Cubic, Cadillac John and Bill Abel, Paul Wine Jones, Mississippi Slim, Little Milton, Bobby Rush, Alvin Youngblood, and Willie King.

Of course, you can't have good blues music without some good food. It's a law or something. So, while the music thrums your soul, blue smoke wafts into your nostrils, bringing the tantalizing aroma of pig meat being roasted on dozens of homemade barbecue pits. Its taste is the flavor of the South.

Held annually in June.

HOG WILD IN CORINTH • CORINTH

Did we mention that barbecue is the flavor of the South? Every year in downtown Corinth, they try to answer that age old question: Who makes the best 'cue? This contest pits professional chefs and backyard 'cuers from all over the state in a cook-off. The winner goes to the cook-off to end all cook-offs, the Memphis in May BBQ Festival cook-off.

Everywhere you'll find serious folks, tending their pigs, turning them at the precise moment and sopping on tangy marinades and sauces. Your mouth won't stop watering from the moment you step into the park until you walk out. But, don't worry, there's plenty of 'cue to go around. Sample a little of each and see if you agree with the judge's decision. In between samples, you can enjoy the wonderful carnival atmosphere, complete with rides and live entertainment.

Held annually in October.

> Mississippi is known as the Magnolia State, for the large number of magnolia trees that perfume her summers. The magnolia is the official state tree and its blossom is the official state flower. The state is also known as the Mud-Cat state, for the proliferation of catfish farms, and the Eagle State, a name that derives from the state coat of arms, which depicts a Bald Eagle clasping arrows and an olive branch in its talons.

HUMMINGBIRD MIGRATION CELEBRATION • HOLLY SPRINGS

Anyone who's watched them will tell you that hummingbirds are fascinating creatures. Hang feeders on your deck or plant some of their favorite flowers in your garden, and your summers will automatically be brightened by their dive-bombing antics.

Look close enough, and you'll see a long tongue whip in and out as they sip the nectar you've provided. Most times, you're rewarded by chirping, a quick "thank-you," perhaps. They're curious little animals, sometimes flitting in to hover in front of you, head cocking from side to side, as if checking out this strange creature that always seems to be watching them.

The Hummingbird Migration Celebration at the Strawberry Plains Audubon Center in Holly Springs is an opportunity to spend the day watching thousands of ruby-throated hummingbirds as they flit in and around the myriad of feeders and native flowers located on the twenty-five hundred acre preserve. The celebration takes advantage of the ruby-throats' annual migration, which takes them to warmer climates across the Gulf of Mexico. They return to North America every spring.

With more than four thousand visitors, the Hummingbird Migration Celebration is one of the largest Audubon-sponsored festivals in the country.

INTERNATIONAL BALLET COMPETITION • JACKSON

Who would have thought that little ol' Jackson would ever become the center of the world of tutus and toe shoes and muscular men in tights? But it happens once every four years, when the USA International Ballet Competition brings the world's premiere ballet dancers to Jackson.

When it began in Jackson in 1979, competitions were held in only three other cities in the world—Varna, Bulgaria; Moscow, Russia; and Tokyo, Japan. In 1982, the U.S. Congress passed a Joint Resolution designating Jackson as the official home of the USA International Ballet Competition. Well, everybody's gotten in on the act these days, with international competitions held in numerous cities. Jackson, however, remains one of the oldest and most respected competitions in the world.

Funny Happenings Here

The two-week USA International Ballet Competition is the Olympics for ballet dancers, where soon-to-be stars compete for gold, silver, and bronze medals, cash prizes, and scholarships. And, like the Olympics, their performances here can make or break them in the world of ballet.

In conjunction with the beautiful and athletic performances of the competition, the USA IBC has become a major dance festival, offering art and costume exhibits, dance workshops, a school for students and teachers, performances by nationally-recognized dance companies, and a showcase performance by Regional Dance America companies.

JUNETEENTH CELEBRATION • COLUMBUS

This celebration came about because of a bit of heinous obfuscation by some greedy Texas plantation owners who didn't want to lose their slave labor. President Abraham Lincoln signed the Emancipation Proclamation, which freed the slaves, on January 1, 1863, but word of the proclamation didn't reach Texas until June 1865. Legend has it that the bearer of the news rode a very slow mule all the way, and that's why it took two years for the news to reach Texas. Yeah, right. Historians know that many slave owners knew of the proclamation but refused to tell their slaves.

There's no stopping progress, however, and so finally, on June 19, 1865, Major General Gordon Granger stood on the balcony of Aston Villa in Galveston and read the proclamation declaring slaves to be free and equals to their owners.

June 19th—Juneteenth for short—immediately became a

day of celebration for African-Americans in Texas until the Civil Rights Movement in the 1960s. It once again became popular in the 1970s.

The Juneteenth Celebration in Columbus is a two-day celebration of the event. There's food, music, and lots of fun, including a softball tournament, children's activities, and events for seniors.

Held annually in (when else?) June.

MAL'S ST. PADDY'S PARADE AND FESTIVAL • JACKSON

What began more than twenty years ago as a way to celebrate St. Patrick's Day and raise a little money for the local hospital has morphed into a giant parade, the country's fourth largest, and a three-day party-fest, with more than 50,000 wild and crazy green-wearing partiers participating.

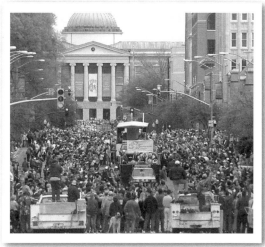

Thousands flood the streets of Jackson for Mal's St. Paddy's Parade and Festival.
Courtesy of Mississippi Development Authority/Division of Tourism.

The whole thing was the idea of Malcolm White,

a prominent Irish-blood Jacksonian, who believed his hometown needed a little fun. OK, it needed a lot of fun. He called up a few friends and got the ball rolling, and it just kept on rolling.

One reason the event has become so popular in recent years is the participation of the wildly popular Sweet Potato Queens. It was in the very first Mal's celebration that Jacksonian Jill Conner Browne first posited her idea. When Mal invited her to enter a float in the parade, she announced she would come as the Sweet Potato Queen. Twenty years later, her series of books about the red-haired, mini-skirted Sweet Potato Queens became a national success story. Today, Sweet Potato Queens from around the country flock to Jackson to celebrate with their mentor and hero. Saving the best for last, the Sweet Potato Queens' fluffy float brings up the rear of the parade.

In addition to the main parade of fifty floats, there's a pet parade, a children's parade and festival, and a huge street festival for you big folks. Wear green. You'll be dancin' a jig in no time.

Held annually in March.

MISSISSIPPI GULF COAST KITE FEST • LONG BEACH

You'll enjoy the high-flying activities at the Mississippi Gulf Coast Kite Fest. You'll learn everything there is to know about flying kites, with master flyers showing off their techniques and demonstrating their prowess in a kite-flying competition and a beautiful kite ballet. Kids will enjoy the opportunity to make their own kites and then participate in the Kid's Kite Run and the Candy Drop. It's lots of fun for the whole family.

Held annually on the last weekend in April.

MULLET FESTIVAL • GAUTIER

The highlight of this fishy festival is the Mullet Toss, where scores of competitors line up to see who can toss a smelly mullet the farthest. And they take their competition seriously, with men's, women's, and children's divisions.

The Mullet Toss isn't the only reason this celebration of coastal traditions and heritage is so popular, however. The festival highlights the work of local artisans with more than sixty-five booths. There are thirty-five heritage areas, and plenty of food vendors (Yes, mullet is on the menu.). In addition, there're children's activities, an antique car show, and a large entertainment schedule with live music and dancing in the streets.

NATIONAL ANVIL SHOOTING CONTEST • LAUREL

It doesn't get much stranger but truer than this! It's amazing what boys can come up with when they've got too much time on their hands. This "sport" supposedly dates back to Civil War days, when those Yankees blundered through, destroying everything in their paths. According to legend, in destroying Southern metal works, they devised a little game where they placed a load of gun powder beneath blacksmiths' anvils and tried to blow them up. All they succeeded in, of course, was blasting them up into the air. The things are made of steel. You can't hurt 'em!

Fast forward to modern days and good ol' boys with nothing to do. Hey, guys. Let's see if we can blow up that anvil! And, voilà, the sport of anvil shooting was born. At first there was just the traditional way of blowing up an anvil: Take an anvil and place no more than two pounds of powder in the little concave space on the bottom. Add a short fuse. Put another anvil—one that weighs no more than one hundred pounds—on top of the base anvil. Light the fuse and run like heck. Boom! The anvil flies into the air, reaching heights of up to one hundred feet. Folks came from several states, and soon a real life anvil-shooting contest evolved.

But, wait! That macho need to soup things up spawned the Super-Modified class, where competitors are allowed to make their own anvils to improve on height and trajectory. And improve they have. The current world record holder blasted his Super-Modified anvil four hundred feet into the air.

OK, we gotta admit that blowing things up holds some attraction. Others agree. In anvil-shooting contests around the country even a few dignitaries have gotten into the act. Folks such as U.S. Senator Lamar Alexander, Ambassador Howard Baker, Senator Nancy Kassabaum, and Four-star General Carl Steiner.

The National Anvil Shooting Contest is held in Laurel every April. But attend at your own risk. Some of those anvils have been known to blow apart. Keep your distance and listen for the famous last words of a Mississippi boy with too much time on his hands: "Hey, y'all. Watch this!"

Pieces and Strings • Port Gibson

Quilting, of course, was born of necessity—a need for something to provide warmth on cold winter nights. But women took pride in their work, producing coverlets that were as much a work of art as a utilities. In earlier times, the making of those quilts was often turned into a social event. Women would come together for a "quilting," later called a "quilting bee." While they worked, they shared family news, exchanged recipes, and, women being what they are, probably discussed men. While some quilted, others would cook a big meal that would be shared by all later.

Today, of course, you can run down to the store for all the warm covers you need, negating the need for quilting. Today's quilters are artisans, helping to keep alive this tradition of beauty. Mississippi Cultural Crossroads, a Claiborne County arts agency dedicated to promoting African-American artists, brings together a group of mostly African-American quilters to celebrate the traditional quilting heritage. The group, sometimes working individually, other times as a group, produces one-of-a-kind quilts that are displayed and sold through Mississippi Cultural Crossroads.

Every year, Mississippi Cultural Crossroads sponsors "Pieces and Strings," a quilting contest for Mississippi quilters. Judged by recognized quilting experts, the quilts are displayed and many are for sale. Several forms of performing arts are also presented at this time.

Held annually in March.

SLUGBURGER FESTIVAL • CORINTH

EEEWWW! You mean people really eat slimy snail burgers? Wait, the snails of Corinth are safe. Slugburgers are made of beef. Well, sorta. See, back during the Depression, beef was scarce. So vendors added fillers, such as cereal, flour, potatoes, cornmeal, and soybeans. They made up small patties of the mixture, deep fried 'em and sold them for a nickel, which was known back then as a "slug."

Since these tasty little artery cloggers originated in Corinth, that town celebrates the tradition with a three-day festival. There's live entertainment, amusement rides, and lots of great food, including the star of the show. They're what you'll get if you order a burger—although you can specify a beef burger, if you prefer.

Held annually in July.

Soulé Live Steam Festival • Meridian

G.W. Soulé missed the boat. To Cuba, that is. So, instead of moving to some foreign country, he founded several businesses in Mississippi, including the Soulé Steam Feed Works, a Meridian-based company that made Spee-D-Twin Steam Engines. When in full operation, the company—in business for 110 years—produced one engine a day, with a total of 4,301 manufactured.

The Soulé Live Steam Festival is held at the Mississippi Industrial Heritage Museum, located inside the refurbished buildings of the Soulé Steam Feed Works. Visitors see operating steam engines from the museum and from around the state. There are demonstrations of blacksmithing, broom-making, and printing. Tours of the museum reveal original machinery and history of the business.

Held annually in October.

Tales from the Crypt • Columbus

Nothing's spookier than nighttime in a cemetery. Trembling in fear, you hear strange, haunting sounds. See wispy tendrils of mist rising at your feet. Feel a cold breath on your neck.

You'll get that delicious shiver of fear during the Tales from the Crypt candlelight tour of Friendship Cemetery, where the spirits of the long buried arise before your very eyes and tell you the tale of their lives. And, interesting lives they were. For Friendship Cemetery is the final resting place of five Confederate generals, two Mississippi governors, and a whole slew of prominent merchants, lawmakers, and authors. You just never know who might appear. Yeah, yeah. We know they're costumed actors, but you're still in a cemetery. At night. Ooo! You just never know what might happen!

Wizard of Oz Festival • Lucedale

Follow the yellow brick road right on over to Lucedale, where they're throwing a *Wizard of Oz* Festival. This two-day extravaganza is filled with Oz-related activities. Sample the pies at Auntie Em's pie booth. Have your picture made with one of the original munchkins. There's bobbing for apples at the Living Apple Trees. You can take a buggy ride—pulled by a horse of another color, of course.

There're parades and hay rides, magicians and costumed characters, a town crier competition and a Dorothy calling contest, a *Wizard of Oz* sing along, and a viewing of the 1939 movie classic. And when you've finally tired yourself out and are ready to go home, you can just click your heels together and say, There's no place like home...

Better watch your step in Strange But True Mississippi. You never know when the long arm of the law may reach out and nab you for breaking one of these strange but true laws!

1. Cattle rustling is punishable by hanging.
2. It is illegal in Mississippi to teach others what polygamy is.
3. In Brandon, it's illegal to attempt to stop someone by parking a motorhome in his path.
4. In Temperance, it's illegal to walk your dog without putting a diaper on him.
5. Living together while not married or having sex with someone you're not married to results in a $500 fine and/or six months in prison.
6. In Tylertown, it's illegal to shave in the center of Main Street.
7. In Truro, a would-be groom must prove himself manly by hunting and killing six blackbirds or three cows.
8. In Alexandria, no man is allowed to make love to his wife with garlic, onions, or sardines on his breath. In addition, if his wife requests it, the law mandates that he must first brush his teeth.
9. It's illegal for a man to be sexually aroused in public.
10. In Oxford, it's illegal to "create unnecessary noises."

The Last Word

As we've mentioned, Mississippi has a truly rich literary heritage, with a list of acclaimed writers as long as the Mighty Mississippi snaking its way across the state. We've already told you about William Faulkner. Here's a little bit about a few more.

LARRY BROWN

Born in Oxford in 1951, Larry Brown is a leading writer of "grit lit." His raw stories of the rural South feature everyday characters dealing with real-life issues, such as alcoholism, suicide, marital strife, and the traumas of war.

Although Brown briefly attended the University of Mississippi, he left without graduating. After a stint in the Marines, he began working in a series of jobs. It was through these jobs, no doubt, that he became familiar with the characters and situations he eventually wrote about.

In 1973, Brown became a firefighter with the Oxford fire department, a job he held until 1990. It was during his life as a firefighter that he began his career as a writer, first publishing stories in magazines and journals. His first book, *Facing the Music*, was published in 1988. It was a collection of pull-no-punches short stories introducing a cast of downtrodden characters. The next year, he published his first novel, *Dirty Work*, inspired by his father's experiences in WWII. When his next book of short stories, *Big Bad Love*, was published in 1990, Brown decided to take up writing full time.

The Last Word

His work has garnered many awards. He was the first two-time winner of the Southern Book Award for Fiction, which he won in 1992 for his novel, *Joe*, and again in 1997 for *Father and Sons*. He was awarded the Mississippi Institute for the Arts and Letters award for fiction, and in 1998, he was the recipient of the Lila Wallace-Reader's Digest Award. In 2000, the State of Mississippi granted him a Governor's Award for Excellence.

Acknowledging that his writing painted a dreary picture of the world, Brown said he couldn't explain why his work was so bleak. "I love living," he said. "And, everything that goes with it." Brown died unexpectedly of a heart attack in 2004. He was just fifty-three.

John Grisham

While John Grisham may not be the first writing lawyer, he is, without a doubt, the most successful. Currently, there are more than 225 million of Grisham's books in print. The books and the movies based on them have been translated or dubbed in twenty-nine languages and have grossed billions.

Born in Arkansas, Grisham came to Mississippi in 1967, at the age of twelve. After realizing his dream of becoming a professional baseball player would never come true, he earned an accounting degree from Mississippi State University then went on to earn a law degree from Ole Miss. He joined a law firm in Southaven, specializing in criminal defense and personal injury litigation. In 1983, he was elected to the Mississippi House of Representatives, where he served until 1990.

One day, Grisham overheard the testimony of a twelve-year-old rape victim in the Dessoto County courthouse and an idea was born. What if, he thought, the girl's father, a black man, had killed the two white rednecks that raped her? And, what if it had all happened in Mississippi during the height of that state's racial strife? And, what if the father was defended by a young white lawyer?

Sounded like it'd make a good book. So, despite the fact that he was working sixty to seventy hours a week as a lawyer, Grisham began to rise at five a.m. every morning to spend several hours writing before going to work. Though rejected several times, *A Time to Kill* was finally published in 1988 with a modest five thousand copy printing.

Immediately upon finishing *A Time to Kill*, Grisham had begun his second book and it was this book—*The Firm*—that began his phenomenal success as a bestselling author. *The Firm* spent forty-seven weeks on *The New York Times* bestseller list and became the bestselling novel of 1991.

Grisham has written a book a year since 1988, and each has been wildly successful. Nine of his books have been turned into movies. Although most of his books have been legal thrillers, he has stepped away from the genre to write *A Painted House* and *Skipping Christmas*, which became the movie *Christmas with the Kranks*. In 1994, he also became publisher—and savior—of the near-destitute magazine *The Oxford American*, located in Oxford.

THOMAS HARRIS

It's Thomas Harris we have to thank for a couple of the most bizarre things in our popular culture: The image of

The Last Word

Anthony Hopkins as Hannibal Lecter wearing that horrific leather mask with the mouth sewn closed and the sipping, slurping sound he made at the thought of eating human flesh.

Thomas Harris was born in 1940 in Jackson, but moved with his family to Rich at a very young age. He grew up here, leaving to attend Baylor University in Waco, Texas, where he was an English major. To help support himself through school, he worked by night as a reporter for the *News-Tribune*.

His first book, *Black Sunday*, was published in 1975. A thriller about a plot to kill thousands with a blimp during a Superbowl, the book was so scary it led to many football stadiums being turned into no-fly zones. It was made into a hit movie two years after publication.

Harris's next book introduced Hannibal Lecter, an evil character who enjoyed dining on human flesh. Titled *Red Dragon*, it was modestly successful and spawned a not-so-successful movie titled *Manhunter*. It was a different situation when he wrote a second book involving the Lecter character, which was published in 1988. When *Silence of the Lambs* was turned into a movie in 1991, it was an instant hit. Starring Anthony Hopkins and Jodie Foster, the movie won all five of the major Academy Award categories, only the third movie to ever do so.

Because of demands from fans, Harris penned a third Hannibal the Cannibal novel, titled simply *Hannibal*, published in 1999. It quickly became a bestseller and the movie of the same name set opening records for box office sales. Continuing to cash in on the character's popularity, a new movie of *Red Dragon*, this time under the original title, was made. And it's not over yet.

Harris penned a prequel to the series, writing the book and the screenplay simultaneously. Titled *Behind the Mask*, the book, published in 2005, gives the story of how Hannibal came to be a cannibal. The movie is scheduled to be released in 2007.

WILLIE MORRIS

Willie Morris said he didn't consider himself a Southern writer. He was, he said, an American writer who happened to come from the South. It's a slim distinction, we say. For Morris's works are Southern. That is, he tells of his personal experiences of the South—the good, the bad, and the ugly. His keen insights into the South's beautiful, but terribly flawed, past and its struggling present could come only from a native Southerner.

Born in Jackson in 1934, Morris moved to Yazoo City when he was six. After graduating valedictorian of Yazoo City High School, he left for the University of Texas at Austin, where as editor of the *Daily Texan*, he quickly angered the Board of Regents with scathing attacks on segregation and censorship. After graduating, he continued his education as a Rhodes Scholar, studying history at Oxford University in England.

He returned to Texas and managed the *Texas Observer*, once again angering folks with his outspoken coverage of controversial issues ignored by the mainstream press, issues such as illiteracy, racial discrimination, the deplorable conditions of nursing homes, and crooked Texan politicians.

From Texas, he moved to New York City, becoming an associate editor of *Harper's* magazine in 1963. Just four years later, he was appointed the youngest ever editor-in-chief of the magazine and immediately set about turning the stogy publication into one of the country's most exciting and influential publications. At about the same time, his first book, *North Toward Home*, was published.

In this autobiography, Morris wrote frankly of growing up in the South in the fifties, a land of grace, of flaws, of cruelty. He wrote of segregation and the rise of Lyndon Johnson in Texas in the fifties and sixties, and of expatriated Southerners, who felt alienated from their states, yet were drawn to them as well. The book became a best seller and won the Houghton Mifflin Literary Fellowship award for non-fiction and several other honors.

Leaving *Harper's* after a dispute with the publication's owners, Morris moved to Bridgehampton, New York, and continued to write—about the South. His next book was *Yazoo: Integration of a Deep-Southern Town* in 1971. He was passionate about racial injustice and this was just one of many of his writings that covered the subject. He also wrote *Good Old Boy*, a book that celebrated his childhood and recounted misadventures of his youth; *The Last of the Southern Girls*, a novel about a Southern debutante in Washington, D.C; and *James Jones: A Friendship*, a book about his friendship with writer James Jones.

In 1980, Morris returned home to serve as writer-in-residence at the University of Mississippi and later moved to Jackson. He continued to write thought-provoking books about the things that were important to him and those were the things that, despite his denials, did make him, indeed, a Southern writer, for they are the things that are engrained in every

Southerner: the importance of family and friends, reverence of the past, and allegiance to a place.

In 2001 his 1993 book, *My Dog Skip*, a remembrance of growing up in the South, was made into a movie. Unfortunately, Morris never saw it. He died of a heart attack in 1999. In 2000, the readers of Jackson's Clarion-Ledger named him Mississippi's favorite non-fiction writer of the millennium.

EUDORA WELTY

The Grande Dame of Southern literature, Eudora Welty was born in Jackson in 1909. She lived the majority of her ninety-two years in her familial homes here. The first home was located on Congress Street. She often rode her bike through the grounds of the state capitol on her way to grammar school. The second home, where she lived until her death in 2001, is located on Pinehurst Street. Willed to the Mississippi Department of Archives and History, the home is a National Historic Landmark and is open to the public as a museum.

Although she had what she described as an idyllic childhood, Welty was known to comment that she had always felt like an outsider in the South—a person standing alone, looking in. Some have speculated this feeling of being an outsider in her hometown may have stemmed from the fact that her parents were transplanted Yankees. I think, instead, feeling like an outsider is the fate of any good writer. It's this standing alone—observing how people live their lives, listening to their voices and hearing their unique language—that gives the ability to re-create those lives in the written word.

The Last Word

Welty began observing and listening early, a fact illustrated in numerous biographies relating that, as a child, she would often sit herself amid a group of her mother's friends and order, "Now talk." As a result, her work displays a pitch-perfect mastery of Southern dialect and culture. Too, her stories and books show an astute understanding of human relationships, particularly the intimate and often strange relationships among families and between men and women.

Her grasp of the human psyche caused much speculation about Welty. In writing about her, many reporters pointedly remarked on the fact that she had never married and had lived practically her entire life in one house. Some even went so far as to speculate on her sex life—well, actually, on whether or not she'd ever had a sex life. The speculation was done, of course, in the name of literary explication. How was it, they asked, that a woman who'd lived her whole life in one Southern town, who'd never married, and who might even have been a virgin, knew so much about the intimacy of human relationships? Imagine the embarrassment these speculations must've caused Welty. Despite her feelings of alienation, she was a genteel Southern woman, with impeccable manners, ever proper and polite, even when refusing to answer the exceedingly rude questions often put to her.

Reading Welty's work brings insights into the human spirit. She parts a curtain, and, like her characters, her readers get a glimpse of some truth that's eluded them, a life they should've had, perhaps, but now never will. She takes you to a place and time that are vaguely familiar, yet somehow strange. And although most of her stories are set in the South with Southern characters, the subjects and relationships she covers are universal.

Recognized as the twentieth century's best short story writer, Welty has won every major literary award except the Nobel. She is a six-time winner of the O. Henry Award for Short Stories and her other awards include the National Medal for Literature, the American Book Award, and the 1972 Pulitzer Prize for her novel *The Optimist's Daughter*.

Eudora Welty has been recognized as the twentieth century's best short story writer.
Courtesy of Mississippi Development Authority/
Division of Tourism.

In addition to writing, she is an accomplished photographer, with two published photography books. During her life, her writing overshadowed her photography, but since her death, that, too, is receiving recognition. It was, she has said, photography that taught her that life doesn't hold still. The need to hold transient life in words is what spurred her to write.

The Last Word

TENNESSEE WILLIAMS

So, how does a guy who was born in the Magnolia State come by the moniker Tennessee? It's simple, really. When Thomas Lanier Williams attended the University of Missouri, his Yankee classmates took to calling him "Tennessee" because of his Southern drawl. Guess Mississippi Williams didn't have quite the same ring to it.

Williams was born in Columbus in 1911 and moved to Clarksdale at age three. His home in Columbus now serves as the Mississippi Welcome Center. In 1918, the family moved to St. Louis, Missouri. With an alcoholic and abusive father, an overbearing mother with dreams of Southern genteel grandeur, and a schizophrenic sister, the Williams family epitomized dysfunctional. They appear, thinly veiled, in many of Williams's most prominent works.

Williams was especially close to his sister, Rose, whom he saw as his muse. Suffering with schizophrenia, she spent much of her life in mental institutions. Despite treatment, she progressed into paranoia, and in 1943, her parents gave consent for a lobotomy that turned out badly. As a result, she was incapacitated for the remainder of her life. Williams was angry about the operation and never forgave his parents for giving their consent.

Williams first gained literary success at the age of sixteen, winning third place (and five dollars) for an essay titled "Can a Good Wife Be a Good Sport?" A year later, "The Vengeance of Nitocris" was published in *Weird Tales*. In the early thirties, he attended the University of Missouri, dropping out before graduating, but not before earning his nickname. In 1935, Williams wrote his first publicly performed play titled *Cairo, Shanghai, Bombay!* which was performed in Memphis, Tennessee.

Continuing to write, he entered the University of Iowa, where he finally received a degree. He won a couple of awards for his writing, but it wasn't until 1944 that he hit the big time with *The Glass Menagerie*, the play many consider his best. This was a year after his sister's botched lobotomy and it's easy to see her as the frail, crippled Laura Wingfield, with his mother serving as the model for Amanda Wingfield, Laura's fading Southern belle mother.

The play started out in Chicago then hit Broadway. It won the New York Drama Critic's Circle Award as the best play of the season and began to establish Williams as one of history's greatest playwrights. In the next eight years, he cinched his place in history with plays such as *A Streetcar Named Desire*, which won the Pulitzer Prize in 1948; *Summer and Smoke; The Rose Tattoo;* and *Camino Real*. With *Streetcar Named Desire* and *The Glass Menagerie* being made into movies, by 1951 he had achieved a fame few playwrights of his time could claim.

For the next thirty years, while dividing his time between his homes in Key West, New Orleans, and New York and sinking deeply into alcoholism, Williams continued to write and pull in critical acclaim and awards, most notably, a second Pulitzer for *Cat on a Hot Tin Roof* in 1955. He also wrote novels, poetry, and short stories.

Oh, yeah, and movie screen plays. His screenplay of the 1956 movie *Baby Doll*, about an unconsummated marriage, was denounced by Cardinal Spellman and the Legion of Decency. *Time* magazine called it "just possibly the dirtiest American made motion picture that has ever been legally exhibited." The shortie pajamas worn by the child bride star of the movie created a new fashion. Maybe you've heard of them? They're called Baby Dolls.

Throughout his life, Williams fought alcoholism and depression, exacerbated by the fear that he would go insane like his sister, Rose. He also suffered the strain of homosexuality in a society hostile to such differences. His work reflected this darkness with a doom that hung over his characters.

In his work, Tennessee Williams pulled back the curtain of Spanish moss obscuring Southern culture and gave the world a glimpse into the eccentricies and dysfunctions that make the American South so poetic and interesting. He not only changed the idea of Southern literature, but also helped paved the way for other Southern writers.

His strange death in New York could've easily been the ending of one of his Southern Gothic plays. At age seventy-one, he was found dead in a room in the Hotel Elysee. The cap of a prescription drug bottle was lodged in this throat. Authorities surmised that, drunk and drugged, he had reached for a pill, but grabbed the bottle cap instead.

what's been passed down to you generationally. Knowing what needs to stay and what needs to go is like digging down to the bedrock before you set your foundation. It's evaluating what needs to stay and eliminating what needs to go. When you fully embrace this process, you will be amazed at what you discover. Then, when the dust settles, the truth remains.

We Want the Truth

We have come a long way together, covering a vast array of ideas about how truth is formed and why it's essential to be clear about what truths we build our values and belief systems upon. This is not the first time the question "What is the foundation of truth?" has been discussed. Truth has been deliberated, dissected, and divided since the beginning of time. People have given the most precious moments of their lives and even lost their lives over discovering the truth.

We have agreed that there are many different worldviews of truth, from empirical truth to convenient truth, objective truth to subjective truth, and normative truth to complex truth. Understanding truth, like food, becomes a part of who we are. We discussed the difference between putting our faith in an object of belief versus the action of belief. We dissected how past influences and future influences are significant factors in how truth is built; but without a strong foundation of truth, the building of our life cannot and will not stand. Thank you for taking this journey with me. Truth in today's world has become so hazy that we've forgotten what a clear picture of truth looks like. This has been my endeavor for this book. My desire is that by understanding truth, my life, your life, and the lives of future generations can live out our purpose and grow to our maximum potential. The road to counterfeits truths is broad and many. The road to the Truth is narrow and few. Understanding truth and why we need it is one thing. To know the Truth is something altogether separate. Since you've come this far with me, I'd like to introduce you to one more truth. This next Truth is the greatest of all realities. Knowing this Truth is the purpose of our existence. When you're ready, turn the page. The door is open. Let's walk through it together.

Chapter 5
Divine Truth

"The truth is incontrovertible. Malice may attack it, ignorance may deride it, but in the end, there it is."

\- Winston S. Churchill

I think that we can now agree that the foundation of our lives must be built on truth. We can also agree that truth can be objective through evidence, and subjective through personal experience. As we search for truth and discover more about truth, we become aware of the complexity of finding truth. The truth seems to be like that proverbial slippery fish on the boat. Up until now, every aspect of truth that we have studied has been about truth that is finite. A finite truth is a truth having bounds or limits; it is measurable. Finite truth is subject to the limitations and conditions of space, time, circumstances, or the laws of nature. For example, gravity as a truth is still subject to the laws of nature. The types of truths we have covered thus far are finite. For us to understand the next truth, it was necessary to lay the foundation for truth. Finite truth is essential for us to function in our day-to-day world.

However, finite truth has limitations because it is conditional on other things. It is limited in its very nature. When you go as far as you can with finite truth, you probably still have questions that need truthful answers. I remember playing in the woods as a young boy, picking up sticks to build a fire. On more than one occasion, I would pick up a stick that I thought was strong, firm, and solid, only to find out it was rotted and hollow inside. I sometimes feel this is the case with finite truth. For some of the more significant, critical questions in life, finite truth feels hollow and weak. I no longer want to build my life on things that feel hollow and weak. I have done that in the past out of a sense of convenience and compliance. In the past, as hard as I tried to bend the laws of nature and turn a finite truth into an infinite truth, I failed. What appeared to be enough and fulfilling only left me dissatisfied, empty, and lost. If the laws of nature limit finite truth, then I needed a truth without limitations. Thus began my quest to see if such truth existed.

Finding such a truth did not happen overnight. And it did not occur without letting go of many of the finite truths that had served me for so long. The thing is, holding onto finite truths was more about comfort than about fulfillment. After all, if one truth